Praise for this new edition of

Introduction to Option-Adjusted Spread Analysis

"Option-adjusted spread analysis is as widely used as it is misunderstood. Tom Miller's update of this fixed-income classic is a paragon of clear thinking and clear writing. **The road to understanding how OAS is computed and implemented begins here.**"

Steven V. Mann, PhD
Professor of Finance, Moore School of Business, University of South Carolina
Coeditor, *The Handbook of Fixed Income Securities*

And praise for the previous edition

"**Lucid and well-written**, *Option-Adjusted Spread Analysis* focuses on the evaluation of put, callable, and sinking fund bonds ... **a top-quality job**."

Derivatives Strategy

"**This introductory book boils each complex concept down to the basics** ... For those who need to know the calculations behind the numbers on their Bloomberg screen, **this is a neat, to-the-point little textbook**: How to determine fair value of bullet and nonbullet bonds, the role of volatility, the binomial tree of short rates, and applications of OAS analysis are some of the subjects covered."

Futures

"Tom Windas opens the black box of option-adjusted spreads. **Practical examples, excellent graphics, and clear explanations** guide the reader to an understanding of bond valuation. Unlike academic discussions of valuation techniques, this book is not just for the 'rocket scientist,' but is **for every investor**."

ANDREW DAVIDSON
President, Andrew Davidson & Co., Inc.
New York

Introduction to
Option-Adjusted Spread Analysis

Also available from
Bloomberg Press

The Credit Default Swap Basis
by Moorad Choudhry

Fixed-Income Securities and Derivatives Handbook: Analysis and Valuation
by Moorad Choudhry

Inside the Yield Book: The Classic That Created the Science of Bond Analysis
by Sidney Homer and Martin L. Leibowitz, PhD

The Securitization Markets Handbook: Structures and Dynamics of Mortgage- and Asset-Backed Securities
by Charles Austin Stone and Anne Zissu, PhD

A complete list of our titles is available at
www.bloomberg.com/books

Introduction to
Option-Adjusted Spread Analysis

Revised and Expanded Third Edition
of the OAS Classic by Tom Windas

Revised by

TOM MILLER

Foreword by PETER WILSON

BLOOMBERG PRESS
NEW YORK

First edition published 1993
Second edition published 1996
Third edition published 2007
1 3 5 7 9 10 8 6 4 2

Library of Congress Cataloging-in-Publication Data

Miller, Tom

Introduction to option-adjusted spread analysis : revised and expanded third edition of the OAS classic by Tom Windas / revised by Tom Miller ; foreword by Peter Wilson.

p. cm.

Summary: "Explains option-adjusted spread analysis, a method for valuing bonds with options. This book takes readers through each step of the calculation"--Provided by publisher.

Includes bibliographical references and index.

ISBN-13: 978-1-57660-241-6 (alk. paper)

ISBN-10: 1-57660-241-9

1. Fixed-income securities. 2. Option-adjusted spread analysis. I. Windas, Tom. Introduction to option-adjusted spread analysis. II. Title.

HG4650.M56 2007
332.63'2283--dc22 2006101298

Dedicated to the curious and those who teach us.

CONTENTS

FOREWORD

THIRTY YEARS AGO, bonds were quoted by coupon and yield to maturity, with the latter widely regarded as a *de facto* total return expectation.

As the bond world evolved, new types of bonds like callables, putables, and later, mortgage-backed securities were invented. This caused a dilemma for investors who were not exactly sure how to measure the risk and return of the new instruments. Or, as a fixed-income investor back in the 1980s might have put it: "Those bonds I purchased in the late 1970s sure paid a wonderfully high coupon, but just when rates went down, the bond was called away, and now I have to reinvest at much lower yields. I wish I could put a value on the option that the issuer retains, to redeem the bonds at par."

The race was on to create methods to measure risk and return that took into consideration the new ways of structuring bonds. One of those methods is called "option-adjusted spread analysis," or "OAS analysis."

Three decades later, the fixed-income market is still known for constantly creating new ways to structure bonds that allow investors to take more types of bets and hedge away more risks than ever before. Most of these new securities involve options, either implicitly or explicitly. The need to understand options therefore grows steadily.

Unfortunately, many market "insiders," including traders, portfolio managers, and researchers, and others who are involved in the markets but do not make their bread and butter there, still lack a thorough understanding of options and therefore are not really comfortable assessing the risk and return of securities with embedded options.

OAS analysis is the method needed to remedy this problem.

This book is useful to everyone who wants to gain a fundamental understanding of option-adjusted spread analysis without earning a PhD in finance. The concepts are presented intuitively, with enough depth to give a solid understanding, but without an overload of formulas. Key concepts like interest rates, volatility, probability, and the interaction between them are presented in a logical, easy-to-follow manner.

As readers of this book will learn, OAS analysis is not a silver bullet or magic formula for fixed-income investing. But it is an important way to measure, manage, and trade risk and return in the marketplace. More than that, it gives market participants a common framework and language to use when buying and selling. This, in and of itself, helps markets become more efficient and liquid, something which benefits most participants.

An important side benefit of learning the fundamentals of option-adjusted spread analysis is that the principles of OAS analysis apply to many markets. Credit, equity, mortgage, and swaption markets all have forms of "optionality" as critical components within them. As such, much presented here will help with evaluating risk in other markets as well.

Happy reading!

—Peter Wilson
Managing Director, Head of Fixed Income Strategy, Americas
Barclays Global Investors

ACKNOWLEDGMENTS

SPECIAL THANKS to all the members of the fixed income and derivatives sales team at Bloomberg, to Peter Wilson of Barclays Global Investors, and to Tom Windas for the care, attention, and craftsmanship of the first edition.

INTRODUCTION

Why OAS Analysis?

INVESTORS USE **option-adjusted spread (OAS) analysis** to first measure the value inherent in a bond's cash flows and **embedded options** and then to compare the results to market reference levels.

This comparative method makes it possible to see how much yield results from what kind of risk. A given bond may pay higher yield for a combination of reasons: there could be increased risk of default or increased uncertainty of cash flows. The bond may have a complex structure or a small market of ready buyers and sellers. The challenge facing those performing valuation of different bonds is to isolate components of risk and ensure adequate compensation for the risk taken.

If different elements of risk and uncertainty can be quantified, the yields of different bond issues can be compared in a meaningful way.

OAS analysis benchmarks the bond's cash flows against reference rates in the market and values the embedded options (calls or puts) versus market volatility. By comparing the components of a given bond's yield with standard benchmarks in a sophisticated way, the investor can clearly identify the relatively cheap or expensive nature of a given price. OAS analysis, when used consistently, provides a market-dependent, apples-to-apples basis for measuring value.

Accomplishing this requires an analytical method suited to the bond's structure. Bonds contain two primary structural elements:

one that determines the payment of interest, another that determines redemption of principal.

In terms of maturity structure, there are two types of bonds: **bullet bonds** and **nonbullet bonds**. Both types pay interest (or coupons) at regular intervals over the life of the bond. They differ in the provisions that govern when principal may be repaid to investors. Bullet bonds repay the full principal amount at maturity, while nonbullet bonds give issuers or investors the right (but not the obligation) to repay (or receive) the principal before the scheduled maturity date. When the bondholder has the right to receive the principal before maturity, the bond is called **putable**. When the issuer has the right to repay principal before maturity, the bond is called **callable**. **Sinking-fund bonds** allow the issuer to pay back portions of the principal to the investors before maturity.

A moment's reflection reveals that nonbullet bonds are inherently less predictable than bullet bonds because doubt about when the contract between the bondholder and the issuer will end is part of the security. Therefore, this uncertainty (optionality) must be accounted for when analyzing nonbullet bonds. A bond with early redemption features should pay a different yield than a similar bond with a firmly stated maturity. And bonds with higher credit (default) risk should pay a different yield than a bond with less credit risk. The challenge is to understand how much of the bond's yield premium is attributable to each type of risk. This is the purpose of option-adjusted spread analysis.

By implementing **option** valuation methods, OAS applications separate these premiums to allow side-by-side valuation of bonds with different redemption structures. This allows identification of bonds that may be mispriced relative to bonds of similar credit and maturity. One can also use OAS tools to understand the implications of volatility in the future values of one's investments. But most important, a buyer or seller can be sure that the pricing is consistent with other observable bonds in the marketplace.

OAS analysis was designed to provide more reliable results than its analytical predecessor, **yield-to-worst analysis**.

Callable and putable bonds are still, today, widely quoted on a yield-to-worst basis. This method, however, contains many assumptions that lead to incorrect valuation. Yield-to-worst analysis assumes that any bond trading above par will be called in the future—but this requires that interest rates in the future stay below the bond's coupon rate—which may or may not occur. Furthermore, yield-to-worst analysis also suggests that the bond will be held to the specified date and all coupons may be reinvested at the calculated yield. This seldom happens for active investors in the bond markets.

On the other hand, OAS analysis uses statistical analysis to make reasonable assumptions about the most likely redemption scenario. This is possible because OAS analysis includes a sophisticated model of the likely **term structure of interest rates**.

Even though the advantages of OAS analysis are well known and OAS computer models are readily available on many electronic trading and information systems, including the Bloomberg Professional service, most fixed-income professionals still use yield-to-worst analysis. Many hesitate to explore OAS analysis because they find the math daunting.

This book is a comprehensive, user-friendly overview of the methods common to almost all OAS models. The book does not delve into complex mathematics or analyze difficult questions in financial engineering; it targets the reader who wishes to better grasp the elements of yield and risk premium in typical bonds available to almost any investor. When finished reading this book, the reader will grasp fundamental valuation of cash flows and embedded options, understand rich-cheap modeling of bond prices, and recognize the inherent flaws in many standard yield quotes he receives today.

The most successful fixed-income investors already use OAS analysis. Anyone who takes the time to understand OAS analysis and to use it in a disciplined way will soon find himself making better buy and sell decisions.

About this Book

LIKE ITS PREDECESSORS, the fundamental objective of this edition of *Introduction to Option-Adjusted Spread Analysis* is to provide a clear description of how OAS analysis handles the vexing problem of evaluating a fixed-income security whose future redemption date and payment stream are influenced by interest rates through the presence of an implicit embedded option.

In presenting the subject matter, basic concepts are presented first and are built upon in a step-by-step fashion. Wherever possible, modeling subtleties unrelated to the concepts and logic underlying the analysis have been omitted in the interest of clarity. As such, this text should not be construed as a comprehensive description of the Bloomberg lognormal OAS or Bloomberg Fair-Value models.

This book includes a glossary. When glossary entries appear in the text they are rendered in **bold** type.

PART ONE

YIELD ANALYSIS VERSUS OAS ANALYSIS

CHAPTER 1

FATAL FLAWS IN TRADITIONAL YIELD CALCULATIONS

TRADITIONAL YIELD CALCULATIONS compare the **yield** of a given bond to the yields of others with similar characteristics, including redemption date, credit rating of issuer, industry, and so forth, and also to a benchmark bond—one considered to be risk free. This is a fairly fruitful way to evaluate bonds with predictable redemption dates (bullet bonds). (It could be argued that other, newer methods are better, but that is the subject of another book.) Unfortunately, yield analysis is often applied to bonds with embedded options (nonbullet bonds). The results of this analysis can be quite unreliable because yield analysis does not account for uncertain redemption dates in a useful way.

This chapter explains yield analysis and identifies how and why employing it on nonbullet bonds can lead to errors.

Yield, Risk, and Benchmarks

Evaluating a fixed-income security means assessing its return, or yield, and the risk it carries. Risk and return are correlated. When investors take a high risk, they expect a high return and vice versa.

By comparing the return of a benchmark bond—most often, a U.S. Treasury since the odds that the U.S. government will default are so low—with the return of the bond being analyzed, it is possible to quantify how much risk one takes in exchange for how much return when making the investment.

The difference between a bond's risk and the risk of its benchmark is called "incremental" risk. The difference in yield between a bond and its benchmark is called **incremental return**, or **yield spread**. When the yield spread increases, so does the incremental risk.

It is important to choose an appropriate benchmark. To do this, consider three variables: coupon (how much interest paid when), **duration** (a measure of the bond's sensitivity to price changes), and maturity date (when the principal is paid back to the investor). The benchmark and the bond being analyzed should have similar coupons, durations, and maturity dates.

When coupon, duration, and maturity date are similar, it is possible to accurately compare the bond's yield with the benchmark's yield.

Calculating Yield

A bond's yield is the return provided by its future cash flows when purchased at a given price. Essentially, a yield calculation solves for the discount rate that present-values these cash flows to a given total present value.

Therefore, calculating the yield of a bond requires a well-defined set of cash flows. This means that all coupon and principal payment dates and amounts must be specified before the yield associated with a given price settlement date can be determined. (This is also why the bonds being compared must have similar coupons, durations, and maturities.)

Once the bond's cash flows are specified, the price-yield calculation shown in **EQUATION 1.1** can be used to calculate the bond's price for a specified yield.

For bullet bonds, the yield calculation is relatively straightforward, because the issue's only possible redemption date is its maturity. This means that the future cash flows contributing to the overall return of the bond are clearly defined. As such, the cash flows to be present-valued in a yield calculation are also clearly defined.

EQUATION 1.1

Price/Yield Equation

$$P=\left(\frac{1}{(1+y/m)^{N-1+T/b}}\right)+\left(\sum_{j=1}^{N}\frac{C/m}{(1+y/m)^{j-1+T/b}}\right)-a$$

Where:

P = Price per dollar of face value

y = Yield to maturity (decimal)

m = Number of compounding periods per year

N = Number of remaining coupon (compounding) dates

T = Number of days from settlement to next compounding date

b = Number of days in the compounding period in which settlement occurs

j = 1

C = Coupon rate (decimal)

a = Accrued interest per dollar of face value

EQUATION 1.1 IS A summation of the present values of a bond's cash flows given a yield rate *y*. This equation can also be used to solve for a bond's yield at a given price. However, since equation 1.1 cannot be rearranged to solve for the yield term *y* explicitly, this quantity must be solved for iteratively. Essentially, an estimate of the yield value is made and an associated price calculated based on the estimated rate. If the calculated price is *greater* than the given price, then the estimated yield value is too low. Similarly, a calculated price *less* than the given price indicates that the yield value is too high. The yield estimate is then adjusted until it converges on the value necessary to match the given price. The result of the calculation is the issue's **yield to workout**, where the workout is the redemption date specified for the bond in the calculation.

The certainty of these cash flows is the crucial component of the validity of the yield analysis. The yield to maturity of a bullet bond, therefore, offers a relevant, objective measure of the return provided by its remaining cash flows for a given purchase price.

Yield Analysis and Nonbullet Bonds

Nonbullet bonds—including putable, callable, and sinking-fund—are not as easy to evaluate. This is because some aspects of their cash flows—such as the timing or the value of their future payments—are uncertain. To show why such issues present obstacles to meaningful yield analysis, the focus will be on the complications posed by callable bonds in particular. However, it should be understood that similar arguments can be extended to putable and sinking-fund issues.

Since callable bonds have more than one possible redemption date (their call dates and maturity), the collection of future cash flows contributing to their overall return is not clearly defined. The uncertainty surrounding such issues' cash flows arises from the fact that their actual redemption dates are unknown ahead of time. Yield calculations for such issues are therefore based on assumed redemption dates.

The implications of an uncertain redemption date are significant. In equation 1.1, the second term represents the summation of the present values of the bond's coupon payments. The number of coupon payments in the summation is directly dependent on the assumed redemption date specified. Yield, which present-values specific cash flows, provides a measure of return based on receiving cash flows through an assumed redemption date. In addition, traditional **price-sensitivity** measures derived from an issue's price-yield relationship, such as duration and **convexity**, are also based on the assumed redemption date.

Furthermore, redemption date assumptions depend on the price used in the analysis: two buyers of the same bond at different prices may expect drastically different redemption dates, thus producing drastically different valuations.

If the actual redemption date of the bond turns out to be different from the assumed redemption date, the collection of cash flows actually received will be different from those included in the analysis. Any return and sensitivity measures based on the assumed redemption date therefore become irrelevant in this situation.

The significance of this shortcoming becomes apparent when it is remembered that an issue's incremental risks are evaluated relative to its incremental return. When the return measure itself is flawed, the possibility of drawing catastrophically incorrect conclusions about risk and return becomes very real.

Yield-to-Worst Analysis

Despite its undesirable properties, yield analysis is routinely used to assess the incremental return of callable bonds. The most common method of evaluating callable securities is on a yield-to-worst basis.

This method selects as the redemption date of a callable bond that which results in the "worst-case" scenario for an investor. For a given price and settlement date, a yield is calculated for each possible redemption date. The particular redemption date associated with the lowest, or "worst," yield is then selected as the assumed redemption date of the bond. All traditional return and sensitivity measures are based in turn on this assumed redemption date.

TABLE 1.1 displays a typical **yields-to-call analysis**, in which the yields to each possible redemption date of a bond are calculated. In this example, the Pacific Bell (AT&T) 6.625 percent bond due 10/15/34 is priced at 100.4500 for settlement on 11/3/06. The lowest yield shown is 6.581 percent and is associated with the 10/15/24 call date. The market therefore assumes, on the basis of the yield-to-worst methodology, that this issue will provide payments until 10/15/24 and will have a duration of 10.395. An investor in this bond would believe he was long a thirteen-year-and-one-month issue and would expect its market value to change by 10.395 percent for a 100-basis-point shift in its yield.

It should be emphasized that the worst redemption date identified by a yield-to-worst analysis is an estimate of the security's redemption date based on current market conditions. The question of when a callable bond will actually be redeemed is not resolved

TABLE 1.1

Yields-to-Call Analysis

Pacific Bell (AT&T) CUSIP: 694032AX1
6.625% Bonds Due 10/15/34

Settlement Date: 11/3/06	Price: 100.4500
Yield to Maturity (10/15/34 @ 100):	6.589%
Yield to Next Call (10/15/13 @ 101.12):	6.671%
Yield to Worst Call (10/15/24 @ 100):	6.581%

Call Date	Call Price	Yield	Adjusted Duration	Risk Factor
10/15/13	101.12	6.671%	5.487	5.530
10/15/14	101.02	6.650	6.092	6.140
10/15/15	100.91	6.633	6.659	6.711
10/15/16	100.81	6.621	7.191	7.247
10/15/17	100.71	6.611	7.689	7.749
10/15/18	100.61	6.604	8.155	8.219
10/15/19	100.51	6.598	8.592	8.659
10/15/20	100.41	6.593	9.001	9.071
10/15/21	100.30	6.589	9.384	9.458
10/15/22	100.20	6.586	9.743	9.820
10/15/23	100.10	6.583	10.080	10.159
10/15/24	100.00	**6.581**	10.395	10.476
10/15/34	100.00	6.589	12.645	12.743

Note: A yields-to-call analysis of the callable Pacific Bell (AT&T) 6.625% bond due 10/15/34 shows the yield to each possible redemption date. At a price of $100.4500, the issue's worst call date is 10/15/24.

SOURCE: BLOOMBERG

by such an analysis. In fact, sufficient changes in the issue's market value can give rise to a new worst redemption date. Such changes are not uncommon and render any return and sensitivity measures based on current redemption estimates misleading.

In **TABLE 1.2**, the same Pacific Bell (AT&T) bond has appreci-

TABLE 1.2

Yields-to-Call Analysis

Pacific Bell (AT&T) CUSIP: 694032AX1
6.625% Bonds Due 10/15/34

Settlement Date: 11/3/06	Price: 103
Yield to Maturity (10/15/34 @ 100):	6.393%
Yield to Next Call (10/15/13 @ 101.12):	6.217%
Yield to Worst Call (10/15/13 @ 101.12):	6.217%

Call Date	Call Price	Yield	Adjusted Duration	Risk Factor
10/15/13	101.12	**6.217%**	5.517	5.701
10/15/14	101.02	6.241	6.128	6.332
10/15/15	100.91	6.259	6.701	6.924
10/15/16	100.81	6.274	7.238	7.479
10/15/17	100.71	6.287	7.742	8.000
10/15/18	100.61	6.298	8.215	8.489
10/15/19	100.51	6.308	8.659	8.947
10/15/20	100.41	6.317	9.075	9.377
10/15/21	100.30	6.324	9.466	9.781
10/15/22	100.20	6.330	9.832	10.160
10/15/23	100.10	6.337	10.176	10.515
10/15/24	100.00	6.342	10.498	10.848
10/15/34	100.00	6.393	12.822	13.249

Note: Because the Pacific Bell (AT&T) issue has many possible call dates, the worst call at any given time corresponds to the lowest yield associated with a given price. A significant change in price can alter the worst date. The price of the bond was raised by 3 points, from 100 to 103, and the worst call date changed from 10/15/24 to 10/15/13.

SOURCE: BLOOMBERG

ated in price from 100.45 to 103. Note, however, that at this new price the lowest yield is 6.217, and the associated redemption date is 10/15/13. In other words, as a result of the issue's three-point price increase, the market now assumes that it will provide cash flows only until its 10/15/13 call date. This reduction in the expected cash flows makes the bond less attractive, since it is now assumed that twenty-one years' worth of the initial payment stream will not occur.

Accordingly, the issue's duration decreases, making it less sensitive to further declines in rates. The investor would be disappointed to find that the market now values his investment as a seven-year issue with a duration of 5.517. If he had hedged his purchase on the basis of its initial 12.161 duration with noncallable benchmark bonds, he would now find that he was significantly **overhedged**—that is, short the market—and would suffer losses from any further declines in rates.

In reality, predicting a future redemption date for a callable bond is tantamount to predicting future interest-rate environments, a task containing obvious inherent uncertainty. This uncertainty may well represent the most significant risk associated with a callable bond, surpassing even the credit risk of the issuer.

Yield measurements ignore this risk by requiring the specification of an assumed redemption date before calculating a rate of return. Once a date is specified, the yield measurement provides an indication of return only to that redemption date.

Even if the assumed redemption date turns out to be correct, this fact will not be known until shortly before redemption. As a result, significant uncertainty will continue to surround the issue during most of its life.

A more complete measure of return should fulfill the following requirements:

1 It should account for the risks posed by an uncertain redemption date by providing an objective measure of performance that is independent of any assumed redemption date.

2 It should provide a means of assessing the incremental return contained in the security relative to a riskless benchmark.

As the following chapters will show, the alternative return measurement method that satisfies these requirements is option-adjusted spread, or OAS, analysis.

CHAPTER 2

THE BOND AS A PORTFOLIO

THIS CHAPTER BEGINS the discussion of option-adjusted spread (OAS) analysis by describing how it handles the early-redemption provisions of a bond. Unlike yield analysis, OAS analysis does not attempt to predict a bond's likely redemption date. Instead, it treats a bond's early-redemption provisions—whether puts, calls, sinking funds, or a combination of the three—as options on its cash flows. Since such provisions are built into the cash-flow structure of a bond, they are referred to as the embedded options of a bond. *Specifically, the OAS model measures the issue's spread, in basis points, relative to risk-free rates of return, after adjusting for the effects of any embedded options.*

Embedded options do not actually exist separate from the issue. They are **hypothetical options** whose behavior replicates that of the early-redemption features of a bond.

Treating a bond's put, call, or sink provisions as embedded options allows us to use **option-valuation models** to assess the impact of such provisions on a bond's value. Since this spread represents the incremental return of the bond, it is conceptually similar to yield spread as discussed in Chapter 1. In both instances, the spread says nothing about whether the bond is rich, cheap, or appropriately priced; instead, it measures the extent to which the issue's expected rate of return exceeds risk-free returns. Ultimately, it is the investor who must decide whether the magnitude of such incremental returns provides adequate compensation for the risks contained in the bond.

The Basic Attributes of Options

Before discussing how a given redemption provision is structured as an option, the basic attributes of options themselves will be reviewed. Fundamentally, an option is a contract. In exchange for a sum of money, referred to as the **option premium**, the seller of the option contract grants the buyer the *right*, not the obligation, to buy or sell an underlying instrument, such as a bond, at a specified price during a specified period. An option that grants the holder the right to buy the instrument is known as a "call" option; one conveying the right to sell is called a "put." The option seller, or writer, is *short* the contract; the buyer is *long*. If the owner elects to exercise the option and enter into the underlying trade, the option writer is obligated to execute according to the terms of the contract.

The price at which the option specifies that the underlying instrument may be bought or sold is referred to as the **exercise**, or **strike**, **price**. An option's **expiration date** defines the last day on which it may be exercised—that is, the last day on which the transaction described in the contract can be executed. Options that can be exercised anytime up to and including the expiration date are called **American options**. Those that can be exercised only on the expiration date are called **European options**. **Bermudian option** structures contain a series of calls coincident with interest payment dates.

OAS analysis treats a bond with early-redemption provisions as a portfolio containing an underlying bullet bond that carries the coupon and maturity date of the actual bond and a put or call option on this underlying issue. The precise option modeled depends on the type of bond being evaluated. This chapter will consider two broad categories of bond structures: putable bonds and callable bonds. Sinking-fund bonds will also be looked at, but in less detail.

Putable Bonds

A putable bond gives the holder the right to sell, or put, the bond back to the issuer before its stated maturity. Thus, the investor, not the issuer, has control over whether the bonds are put back. The prospectus specifies the price and time period for exercising the put.

In general, an owner of a putable bond will exercise this option when the security's value is threatened by adverse circumstances, such as rising interest rates or a downgrade in the issuer's credit standing. (If a downgrade is sufficiently large, however, the onslaught of investors exercising their puts may exceed the issuer's ability to redeem the bonds. In this case, a put would provide little protection against the erosion of principal value.)

Because typical OAS analysis is interest-rate dependent, it does not consider non–interest-rate-influenced behavior resulting from such things as "poison" puts or puts exercised because of credit collapse. However, since the analysis does handle all interest-rate-sensitive elements, the OAS-modeled portfolio's exercise of the put option in a rising-interest-rate environment would replicate the behavior of the actual bond.

Exercising the put during a period of rising interest rates provides bondholders with two benefits: First, investors avoid declines in the bond's market value below the put price, and, second, the dollar proceeds from the redemption can be reinvested in an issue with similar credit risk and a higher rate of return or with superior credit and returns similar to those currently being received. From this standpoint, a put provision acts as a floor, or lower limit, to the bond's market value and is therefore considered beneficial to bondholders.

As an example, consider the International Paper Company 7.2 percent bond due November 2026. The cash-flow attributes of this bond, shown in **TABLE 2.1**, indicate that its fixed 7.20 percent coupon is paid semiannually, on the first of May and November, until its stated maturity on 11/1/26. In addition, it contains a put provision that allows bondholders to put the bonds back to International Paper at a price of 100, or **par**, on 11/1/11, a single day fifteen years before maturity.

TABLE 2.1

Cash-Flow Description

International Paper Company
7.2% Putable Bond Due 11/1/26

Maturity:	11/1/26
Coupon:	7.200%
Payment Frequency:	Semiannual
Payment Dates:	5/1 and 11/1
Put Date:	11/1/11 only
Put Price:	100-00

Note: A description of the International Paper Company putable bond. Bondholders have the option to sell, or put, this bond back to the issuer at par on 11/1/11.

SOURCE: BLOOMBERG

OAS analysis models this putable bond as a portfolio containing a bullet-bond position and an option position. Owners of the bond are entitled to receive its coupon and principal cash flows and therefore are considered to be *long* an underlying bullet issue with the actual bond's 7.20 percent coupon and 11/1/26 maturity. Since owners of the actual bond have the right to put it back to the issuer on 11/1/11, they are also considered to be *long* a put option on the underlying bullet. This is modeled as a European put option (since it can be exercised only on a single day) with a 11/1/11 expiration and a strike price of 100. Thus, OAS analysis treats the owner of a put bond as having a long position in an underlying bullet issue and a long position in a put option on the bullet.

Callable Bonds

Issuers of callable bonds retain the right to buy, or call, their bonds from bondholders before the stated maturity. In this case, it is the issuer, not the bondholder, who has discretion over whether the early-redemption provision is exercised. As in the previous example, the details of the call structure are given in the bond's prospectus. Issuers generally call such bonds when declining interest rates enable them to replace borrowed capital at a lower coupon rate. The threat of early redemption under circumstances that would normally benefit a bondholder limits a callable bond's ability to appreciate in value. This limit acts as a cap, or upper limit, on the bond's market value.

Callable bonds are typically structured in one of two broad formats, referred to as **discretely callable** and **continuously callable**. A discretely callable bond may be called only periodically—for example, on semiannual coupon dates over a portion of the issue's life—usually at par. Continuously callable bonds become eligible for call, generally at par, some number of years before maturity and remain callable until maturity.

As an example of a continuously callable bond, consider the Federal National Mortgage Association (Fannie Mae) 5 percent bonds due June 24, 2020. **TABLE 2.2** shows that this issue pays a

TABLE 2.2

Cash-Flow Description

Federal National Mortgage Association
5% Callable Bond Due 6/24/20

Maturity:	6/24/20
Coupon:	5%
Payment Frequency:	Monthly
Payment Dates:	24th of each month
Call Dates:	Continuously from 6/24/08 until maturity
Call Price:	100-00

Note: A description of a Fannie Mae callable bond. The issuer has the option to buy, or call, this bond away from investors at par on 6/24/08 or any day thereafter.

SOURCE: BLOOMBERG

fixed 5 percent monthly coupon, has a stated maturity on 6/24/20, and is continuously callable at par starting on 6/24/08.

OAS analysis models this bond in a manner similar to that used in the putable-bond example. Once again, owners of the actual bond are entitled to receive its coupon and principal cash flows and therefore are considered to be long an underlying bullet having a

TABLE 2.3

Cash-Flow Description

Pacific Bell (AT&T) CUSIP: 694032AX1
6.625% Callable Bond Due 10/15/34

Maturity:	10/15/34
Coupon:	6.625%
Payment Frequency:	Semiannual
Payment Dates:	4/15 and 10/15

Call Date	Call Price
10/15/13	101.12
10/15/14	101.02
10/15/15	100.91
10/15/16	100.81
10/15/17	100.71
10/15/18	100.61
10/15/19	100.51
10/15/20	100.41
10/15/21	100.30
10/15/22	100.20
10/15/23	100.10
10/15/24	100.00
10/15/34	100.00

Note: An example of a continuously callable bond with declining premium call prices. Each call price is in effect from its call date to the next call date.

SOURCE: BLOOMBERG

5 percent coupon and 6/24/20 maturity. However, since the issuer of the actual bond has the right to call it away from investors, it is the issuer who is long, and investors who are short, a call option on the bond's cash flows. This is modeled as an American call option (since it can be exercised anytime up to and including expiration) that goes into effect on the first call date, 6/24/08, expires on 6/24/20, and has a strike price of 100. Thus, OAS analysis models a continuously callable bond as a portfolio containing a long position in an underlying bullet issue and a short position in an American call option on the bullet.

Instead of beginning and remaining at par, the strike prices of calls on many bonds start at a premium price and decline to par over time. The Pacific Bell (AT&T) 6.625 percent bond due in October 2034, shown in **TABLE 2.3**, illustrates this type of call feature. In this case, the call price is a function of time: 101.12 from 10/15/13 to 10/15/14, 101.02 from 10/15/14 to 10/15/15, and so on, until 10/15/24 through maturity when the bond is callable at par. OAS analysis models this bond as a portfolio containing a long position in an underlying bullet and a short position in a call option with a strike price that declines over time.

Regardless of the specific nature of the calls, owners of callable bonds are short the embedded call option on the underlying bond's cash flows. Issuers, who are long these calls, will exercise them when it is to their advantage to do so.

Sinking-Fund Bonds

Sinking-fund bonds contain provisions for an issuer to sink, or retire, portions of their principal periodically before maturity on a mandatory and/or voluntary basis. The prospectus specifies the timing and pricing of the sinks. Mandatory sink provisions dictate the amount that an issuer must redeem at designated times; a voluntary sink provision gives the issuer discretion over how much is redeemed at these times.

The treatment of sinking-fund bonds can be quite complex, since many factors contribute to their value and the manner in which they trade. However, some generalizations about the behavior of these issues can be made by assuming that in a given sink period, an issuer will be faced with a mandatory sink requirement that has not been previously satisfied.

If the sinking-fund bond is trading at a premium price, the sink will act as a partial call, because the issuer can retire the mandatory amount at a lower sink price, usually par, on a lottery or pro rata basis. If, instead, the bonds are trading at a discount, the sink's behavior is determined by how the issue is distributed among investors. If there are many different investors, the issuer can satisfy the mandatory sink requirement by purchasing the issue at a discount in the market. The sink then acts like a partial call with a discount strike price. However, if relatively few investors have "collected" the issue, they can force the issuer to pay an inflated price, and the sink will act like a put. For those sinking-fund bonds whose sinks must be redeemed at par, the sink acts like a call if the bond is trading at a premium and like a put if the bond is trading at a discount.

The manner in which a voluntary sink provision is administered by an issuer can complicate the evaluation of a sinking-fund issue. For example, an issuer may buy more than the mandatory amount and hold the excess in escrow to satisfy a sink requirement in a future period. This would make the issuer's actions in a future period more difficult for the market to predict.

Valuing the "Portfolio"

Regardless of whether a particular issue contains a put, call, or sinking-fund provision—or elements of all three—OAS analysis treats the structure of a bond as a portfolio containing an underlying bullet bond and option positions. Extending this approach, the analysis treats the value of the bond as the value of its equivalent portfolio. Since the total value of a portfolio is the sum of the values of its individual positions, a bond's value can be viewed as the sum of the values of its underlying bullet-bond and bond-option components. This relationship is expressed algebraically in **EQUATION 2.1**.

Equation 2.1 expresses the equivalency between an actual bond's value and the value of its underlying bullet and option components.

EQUATION 2.1

Equivalency Between an Actual Bond's Value and the Value of Its Underlying Bullet and Option Components

$$B_{ab} = B_{ub} + O$$

Where: B_{ab} = Value of the actual bond
B_{ub} = Value of the underlying bullet bond
O = Value of the embedded option(s)

This relationship must hold for all prices at which the actual bond is valued. Although the emphasis of this analysis is on nonbullet bonds, equation 2.1 is valid for bullet issues as well and can be used to demonstrate that the underlying bullet has to contain the coupon and maturity of the actual bond in order for the equivalency to be maintained. In this case, the absence of embedded options means that the option-price component, O, is equal to zero, so that the value of the actual bond is simply equal to that of its underlying bullet. The only way this equivalency can be maintained for all prices is if the actual and underlying bullet bonds are identical in every way—namely, coupon rate and maturity date. Since equation 2.1 must be valid for both bullet and nonbullet bonds, it forms the framework for evaluating bonds with dissimilar cash-flow structures on a comparative basis.

As already stated, an embedded put option is a beneficial attribute of a bond's structure that contributes to the issue's value by acting as a floor on its price. Thus, the greater the value of the put, the greater the value of the putable bond. The general relationship expressed in equation 2.1 can be rewritten to reflect this condition as **EQUATION 2.2**.

Equation 2.2 states that the value of a putable bond is equal to the sum of the values of the underlying bullet and embedded put option. If either of these components were to increase in value,

EQUATION 2.2

Putable-Bond Equivalency

$$B_{pb} = B_{ub} + P$$

Where:
B_{pb} = Value of the actual putable bond
B_{ub} = Value of the underlying bullet bond
P = Value of the embedded put option

then—all else being equal—the value of the putable bond would increase as well.

Callable bonds, on the other hand, are modeled with a short position in an embedded call option that acts like a cap on the actual bond's value. Because the value of a short position is value owed to someone else, it reduces the value of the actual bond's equivalent portfolio. Therefore, the value of a short embedded call reduces the value of a callable bond. This relationship is expressed in **EQUATION 2.3**.

Equation 2.3 states that a callable bond is equal to the price of the underlying bullet less the price of the embedded call. Therefore, if the value of the call option were to increase, the value of the callable bond would decrease (all else remaining unchanged).

EQUATION 2.3

Callable-Bond Equivalency

$$B_{cb} = B_{ub} - C$$

Where:
B_{cb} = Value of the actual callable bond
B_{ub} = Value of the underlying bullet bond
C = Value of the embedded call option

As the preceding examples have shown, embedded options play an important role not only in the behavior of a bond but in its valuation as well. One reason yield analysis is inappropriate for nonbullet bonds is that it completely ignores the option component, or optionality, of a bond's value by treating it as a bullet issue with an assumed redemption date.

PART
TWO

VALUING OPTIONS

CHAPTER 3

INTRINSIC VALUE

CHAPTER 2 HIGHLIGHTED the importance of the embedded-option component of a bond. This chapter first focuses on how **option value** is described and then sets the stage for the quantitative methods employed in option-adjusted spread (OAS) analysis.

An option's price is composed of two components, referred to as **intrinsic value** and **time value**.

Intrinsic Value

Intrinsic value quantifies the profitability of exercising an option immediately, and is measured as the difference between the option's strike price and the current market price of the underlying instrument. As an example, consider an investor, A, who owns both a bullet bond with a market price of 98 and a par (100) put on this bond that is currently exercisable. If the investor exercised the put option and sold the bond at the 100 strike price to the put writer, he would receive a cash value two points *greater* than he would receive if he sold the bond in the market at 98. Thus, the put option has an intrinsic value of (100 – 98 =) two points.

As another example, consider an investor, B, who buys a bond at par and simultaneously sells to investor C a call option on this bond with a 101.875 strike price. Assume that, some time later, investor B's bond is trading with a market price of 104.375. At that time investor C, wishing to own the bond, has the choice of buying it in the market at 104.375 or calling it away from B at 101.875. Given these alternatives, C would exercise his option and purchase the bond from B, saving himself (104.375 – 101.875 =) 2.5 points on the bond's cost. This 2.5-point advantage is the intrinsic value of the call option. In this case, investor B is short the intrinsic value because he is short the call.

Options that contain intrinsic value are said to be **in the money**. If the strike price is equal to the underlying instrument's market price, the option is said to be **at the money**. A call option is **out of the money** if its strike price is above the market price of the underlying security, whereas a put option is out of the money when its strike price is below the market price. At-the-money and out-of-the-money options contain no intrinsic value.

Time Value

In general, an option's total value, or premium, will exceed any intrinsic value it may contain. The difference between an option's total value and its intrinsic value is its time value. Options without intrinsic value, such as out-of-the-money options or options not currently exercisable, have premiums composed entirely of time value. Whereas intrinsic value describes an option's current profitability associated with an immediate exercise, time value describes an option's expected profitability associated with exercise on a future date. Essentially, this portion of an option's total worth represents the market's opinion on the value of a "bet" that the option may be profitably exercised in the future. All else being equal, in-the-money options are more valuable than at-the-money options, which in turn are more valuable than out-of-the-money options. The principles used to determine this value will be discussed in greater detail in Chapter 4.

Total Value

Having defined the two components of option value in general terms, we can express the relationship between an option's total value (premium) and its intrinsic and time values as **EQUATION 3.1**.

EQUATION 3.1

Option-Value Components

$$O = o_i + o_t$$

Where:

O = Total value of the option

o_i = Intrinsic value of the option

o_t = Time value of the option

The relationship expressed in equation 3.1 can be substituted for the appropriate terms in equations 2.2 and 2.3 to show explicitly each of the components that drive the value of putable and callable bonds. Equation 2.2, for putable bonds, is rewritten as **EQUATION 3.2**, and on the next page, equation 2.3, for callable bonds, as **EQUATION 3.3**.

EQUATION 3.2

Putable-Bond Components

$$B_{pb} = B_{ub} + (p_i + p_t)$$

Where:

B_{pb} = Value of the actual putable bond

B_{ub} = Value of the underlying bullet bond

p_i = Intrinsic value of the embedded put option

p_t = Time value of the embedded put option

EQUATION 3.3

Callable-Bond Components

$$B_{cb} = B_{ub} - (c_i + c_t)$$

Where:

B_{cb} = Value of the actual callable bond
B_{ub} = Value of the underlying bullet bond
c_i = Intrinsic value of the embedded call option
c_t = Time value of the embedded call option

Equations 3.2 and 3.3 describe the basic components of a non-bullet bond's value as modeled by OAS analysis. Of these, the only quantities directly observable in the market are the prices of the actual putable and callable bonds, B_{pb} and B_{cb}. In theory, one approach to judging the appropriateness of a bond's market value would be to estimate the value of each of the terms on the right side of equation 3.2 or 3.3 independently, combine these values, and then compare the theoretical result with the bond's observed value. A market value greater than the theoretical value would indicate an overvalued, or **rich**, security; a market value less than the theoretical value would indicate an undervalued, or **cheap**, security.

In practice, such an analysis would require rigorous methods for estimating the value of each of the terms in equations 3.2 and 3.3. For example, the value of the underlying bullet could be estimated based on the credit quality of the issuer and the expected future cash flows of the bond. Using this value, the intrinsic value of an immediately exercisable embedded option could be determined. Finally, the option's time value could be estimated based on the market's expectations of the option's future profitability.

CHAPTER 4

TIME VALUE

CHAPTER 3 DESCRIBED an option's total value in terms of its intrinsic and time values. Intrinsic value was said to pertain only to options that may be profitably exercised immediately and was measured as the difference between the option's strike price and the underlying security's current market price. Time value was discussed within the context of the market's view of the expected profitability of exercising the option on a future date.

In general, outstanding nonbullet bonds contain embedded options that possess little or no intrinsic value. This is because bonds with currently exercisable in-the-money options tend to be redeemed by the option holders—issuers in the case of callable bonds and investors in the case of putable bonds. Remaining issues possess embedded options with no intrinsic value because they are either out of the money or are not currently exercisable.

Since most nonbullet bonds contain embedded options that possess no intrinsic value, their option components are composed entirely of time value. Measuring this quantity is therefore crucial to the evaluation of nonbullet bonds and is one of the central issues addressed by option-adjusted spread (OAS) analysis. This chapter will introduce the concepts that govern the measurement of time value. It will show how these same principles are employed to determine the OAS of a bond.

Although several methods for estimating time value exist, they all share the fundamental objective of projecting a rationally arrived-at price distribution for the underlying security out to the future exercise dates of the option. In other words, given a series of rational prices for the underlying bond on an embedded option's future exercise date, the option's expected intrinsic value on that future date may be determined. Once measured, the future intrinsic value is present-valued and referred to as the time value of the option.

Calculating an Option's Time Value

Though the basic approach to measuring time value seems straightforward, putting the concepts into practice is somewhat more involved. To introduce the working principles, this chapter will consider the following process involving the toss of a coin: if the outcome of the toss is heads, the payout is $20; if the outcome is tails, the payout is nothing. In this process, the coin has an equal chance of landing heads or tails up, and the outcome of a given toss is uninfluenced by the outcome of any previous toss.

On any single toss, the only possible outcome is heads, which generates a payout of $20, or tails, which generates no payout. Over

EQUATION 4.1

Expected Payout of a Toss

$$E(w) = \sum_{i=1}^{M}(w_i \times p_i)$$

Where:

$E(w)$ = Expected payout from one toss

w_i = Payout received from an outcome i

p_i = Probability that an outcome i will occur

M = Number of possible different outcomes

i = 1, 2, 3, ..., M

many tosses, the expected outcome would be heads 50 percent of the time and tails 50 percent of the time, leading to an expected payout of $20 on one half of the tosses and $0 on the other. In general, the expected payout of one toss is calculated by weighting the payout associated with each possible outcome by the probability that the outcome will occur. **EQUATION 4.1** expresses this expectation mathematically.

The expected payout from one toss of the coin would therefore be calculated as follows:

$$
\begin{aligned}
E(w) &= \sum_{i=1}^{M}(w_i \times p_i) \\
&= (w_1 \times p_1) + (w_2 \times p_2) \\
&= (\text{payout from heads}) \times (\text{probability of heads}) \\
&\quad + (\text{payout from tails}) \times (\text{probability of tails}) \\
&= (\$20) \times (50\%) + (\$0) \times (50\%) \\
&= \$10
\end{aligned}
$$

This example demonstrates that even though the only outcome of a single toss is either $20 or $0, over many tosses the expected average payout would be $10 per toss. Further, the expected payout from *n* tosses would be *n* times the expected payout of one toss. **EQUATION 4.2** expresses this observation formally.

EQUATION 4.2

Expected Payout of *n* Tosses

$$E(nw) = n \times E(w)$$

Where: $E(nw)$ = Expected payout from n tosses
n = Number of tosses
$E(w)$ = Expected payout from one toss

From equation 4.2, the expected payout from ten tosses would be calculated as follows:

$$
\begin{aligned}
E(10\,w) &= (10) \times E(w) \\
&= (10) \times (\text{expected payout from one toss}) \\
&= (10) \times (\$10) \\
&= \$100
\end{aligned}
$$

Since the coin toss has an expected payout of $10 per toss, it can be said to have "worth." To determine the magnitude of this worth, imagine the choice is between paying today for ten tosses of the coin that will take place one year from now and buying, for $95.18, a risk-free Treasury bill with a face value of $100 that matures in one year. (A one-year term was used to simplify the math. However, at the time of publication, the U. S. Treasury was not issuing one-year bills.)

To contrast these two choices, consider that the payout of ten tosses of the coin, although expected to be $100, is by no means certain. Even though the most probable outcome of these tosses is five heads and five tails, for a total payout of $100, it is possible to have an outcome with less than five heads and, therefore, a payout that is less than $100. The Treasury bill, on the other hand, will pay $100 at maturity with absolute certainty. The difference, then, between these two choices is that the expected payout from the toss contains risk, whereas the certain payout of the bill does not.

The $4.82 profit associated with purchasing the Treasury bill is the difference between its $100 payout at maturity and its $95.18 cost today. This profit is risk-free, meaning that the outlay of $95.18 will result in a definite gain of $4.82. When measured relative to the cost of the investment, the $4.82 gain equates to a bond-equivalent yield of 5 percent. Since this yield is associated with a risk-free investment, it is referred to as a "risk-free rate of return." Given the alternative of this risk-free return, the minimum expected rate of return the purchaser would be willing to accept from the coin toss (assuming he was risk-averse) would be 5 percent, meaning that the maximum he would be willing to pay for ten tosses would be $95.18. If he paid more than this amount, he would be accepting an expected rate of return from a risky investment that was less than the risk-free alternative.

Stated another way, the $95.18 represents the present value of the expected outcome of ten coin tosses, or $100, one year in the future, as determined by the 5 percent risk-free rate. In general, the present value of an expected future payout is determined by the risk-free rate of return for the intervening period.

The coin toss is a popular example of a **binomial process**. In a binomial process, each step, or trial, has only two possible outcomes. A trinomial process would have precisely three possible outcomes. The set of all possible outcomes of *n* trials of a binomial process is referred to as a **binomial distribution** of outcomes. For example, one toss of a coin will have one of two possible outcomes: heads or tails. Each of these outcomes has a one-in-two chance, or a 50 percent probability, of occurring.

Similarly, three tosses of a coin will have one of eight possible outcomes, where H denotes heads and T denotes tails: HHH, HHT, HTH, THH, TTH, THT, HTT, and TTT. Of these eight possibilities, one is all heads (HHH), one is all tails (TTT), three have two heads and one tails (HHT, HTH, and THH), and three have one heads and two tails (TTH, THT, and HTT). Therefore, three tosses of a coin have a one-in-eight chance, or a 12.5 percent probability, of resulting in three heads, a 12.5 percent probability of resulting in three tails, a three-in-eight chance, or a 37.5 percent probability, of resulting in two heads and one tails, and a 37.5 percent probability of resulting in one heads and two tails. These outcomes and their associated probabilities describe the binomial distribution for this three-trial binomial process.

A graphic representation of this process, referred to as a "binomial tree of outcomes," is shown in **FIGURE 4.1** on the next two pages. From point A, the first toss of the coin is made. This toss has a 50 percent chance of resulting in heads, as shown on line AB, and a 50 percent chance of resulting in tails, as shown on AC. Note that the expected outcome of the first toss is a payout of $10, since there is a 50 percent chance of winning $20 and a 50 percent chance of winning $0.

Regardless of the outcome of the first toss, the outcome of the second toss again has an equal chance of being heads or tails. From

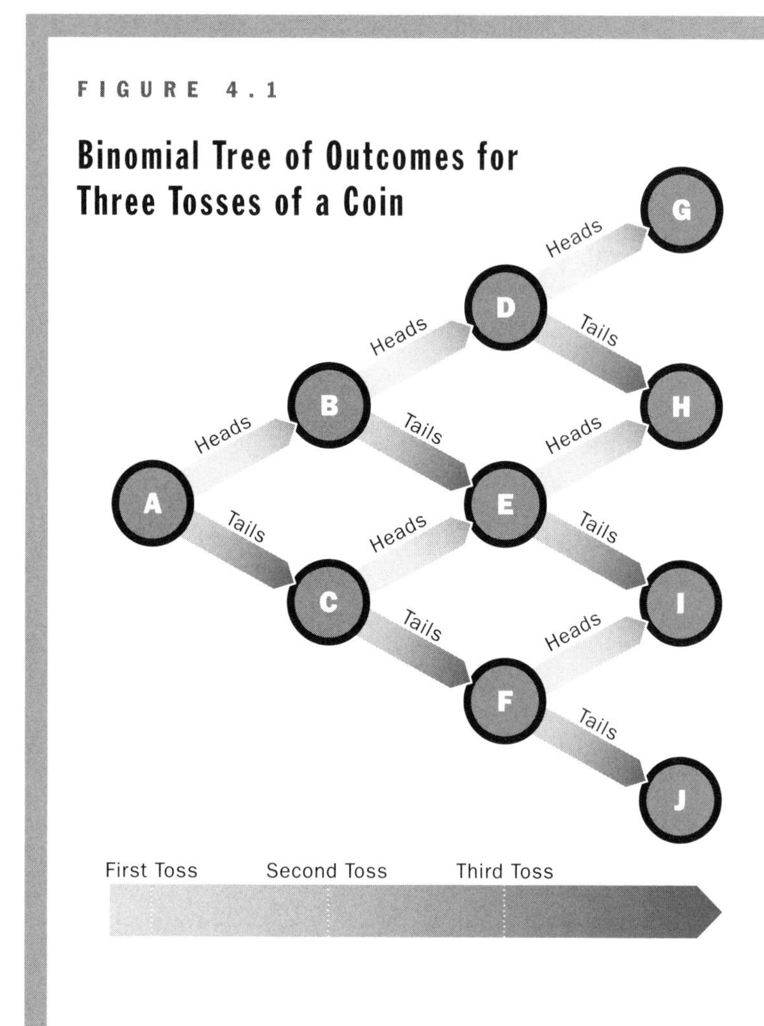

FIGURE 4.1

Binomial Tree of Outcomes for Three Tosses of a Coin

point B, the second toss may have an outcome of heads or tails; similar outcomes are possible from point C. As in the first toss, the expected payout of the second toss is $10. Similarly, the outcome of the third toss, regardless of the outcomes of previous tosses, results in either heads or tails.

	3-Toss Payout	Probability	Expected Payout
G	$60	$^1/_8$	$^{60}/_8$ = $7.50
H	$40	$^3/_8$	$^{120}/_8$ = $15.00
I	$20	$^3/_8$	$^{60}/_8$ = $7.50
J	$0	$^1/_8$	$^0/_8$ = $0.00
			$30.00

Each of the eight possible outcomes listed above is represented by paths in the binomial tree: There is only one way to get three heads (path ABDG), one way to get three tails (path ACFJ), three ways to get two heads and one tails (paths ABDH, ABEH, and ACEH), and three ways to get one heads and two tails (paths ABEI,

ACEI, and ACFI). In addition, of the eight possible outcomes, one path has a payout of \$60 (all heads), three have payouts of \$40 (two heads and one tails), three have payouts of \$20 (one heads and two tails), and one has a payout of \$0 (all tails). The expected payout of three tosses can therefore be calculated by multiplying the number of paths providing a given payout by the value of the payout, adding the results together, and then dividing by the total number of paths. This gives:

$$[(1 \times \$60) + (3 \times \$40) + (3 \times \$20) + (1 \times \$0)] \div 8 = \$30$$

The above result matches the result generated using equations 4.1 and 4.2.

The coin-toss example, along with the binomial tree diagram, provides a simple illustration of many of the properties of a binomial process. The principles that govern such processes form the basis for a popular model frequently used to evaluate options on fixed-income securities. This model, called the **arbitrage-free binomial tree of risk-free short rates**, or the **lognormal model**, is introduced in the next chapter.

PART THREE

Modeling Interest Rates

CHAPTER 5

IMPLIED SPOT AND FORWARD RATES

CHAPTER 4 STATED that an option's time value is determined in three steps:

1 A rational distribution of prices for the underlying security is projected out to an option's future exercise date.

2 The option's intrinsic value on the future date is measured relative to the underlying bond's projected price distribution.

3 Any resulting intrinsic value is present-valued over the intervening period and expressed as the option's time value.

The binomial-tree option model employs many of the principles highlighted in Chapter 4's coin-toss example. *The chief objective of the model is to generate a distribution of future prices for an option's underlying security based on observable market conditions.* It is essential that this be done without incorporating unrealistic assumptions about the underlying instrument's price behavior. (For example, interest rates are unlikely to go negative.)

Perhaps the most significant characteristic of a fixed-income security is that its price varies inversely with interest rates. Moreover, the degree to which a bond's price changes for a given shift in its yield decreases as its duration decreases. In other words, a bond's price sensitivity to changes in interest rates decreases over the course of its life. This property explains why, in general, a given yield shift generates progressively smaller price changes as bond maturities decrease. It would therefore be unrealistic for a fixed-income option model to assume that a bond's ability to achieve a given price change remains constant over the course of its life. As a result, *bond-option models focus primarily on modeling a distribution of interest rates, rather than prices, on an option's future exercise date. Bond prices are then derived from the model's interest-rate distribution.*

THE OBSERVABLE CONDITIONS that serve as the foundation of the model are the annualized rates of return associated with the various risk-free bonds that make up the **benchmark yield curve**. In the U.S. markets, for example, the most recently issued Treasury bills, notes, and bonds may be taken to describe a dollar-denominated benchmark curve. The risk-free rates associated with these issues are employed in a manner similar to the rate in the coin-toss example, in which the present value of an expected future payout was determined. Taken together, these rates describe the term structure of risk-free interest rates.

More recently, market participants have adopted the interest-rate swap curve as a better benchmark. Swap curves provide a set of rates that represent the efficient frontier between fixed and floating rates. The rates are of constant maturity from day to day and are much more correlated to corporate borrowing levels. They are also relatively free of effects from cost-of-carry. (For more on reference curve choices, see the Conclusion.)

In addition to describing the risk-free returns available in the market today, the benchmark yield curve also implies risk-free rates of return for future time periods. These implied future rates, referred to as **implied benchmark forward rates**, are derived from a given **yield curve** and they form the basis for formulating a bond's price distribution on a future date. This chapter will describe how implied forward rates are derived from a benchmark yield curve.

The chief purpose of OAS analysis is to measure the extent to which the expected return of a bond exceeds the risk-free returns

TABLE 5.1

Hypothetical Benchmark Yield Curve for 6/15/06

Benchmark Issue	Years to Maturity	Issue's Coupon	Issue's Maturity	Issue's Observed Price	Issue's Observed Yield
6-month	0.5	6%	12/15/06	100	6.000%
1-year	1.0	7%	6/15/07	100	7.000%
1.5-year	1.5	8%	12/15/07	100	8.000%
2-year	2.0	9%	6/15/08	100	9.000%

available from benchmark securities. Benchmark returns are most often expressed as the yields of the risk-free bonds that constitute the benchmark yield curve. **TABLE 5.1** shows a hypothetical curve for 6/15/06, the date on which an OAS analysis is to be conducted. The observed yields of the benchmark bonds that compose the curve are displayed in the last column. All rates are annualized and assume semiannual compounding.

A bond's yield is the single rate that present-values each of its future cash flows to a given price. Because each cash flow is present-valued at the same rate, bond yields introduce inconsistencies that make them difficult to use in OAS analysis. To see why, consider that all the bonds pictured in table 5.1 pay semiannual coupons on 6/15 and 12/15 of a given year and have exactly the same amount of time—six months—between their valuation date, 6/15/06, and their first coupon payment date, 12/15/06. However, since each issue carries a different yield, each present-values its six-month coupon payment at a different rate. Specifically, the 6-month issue present-values its six-month coupon payment at its 6 percent yield to maturity, the 1-year issue at 7 percent, the 1.5-year at 8 percent, and the 2-year at 9 percent.

Because each of these issues uses a different rate to present-value a cash flow occurring at the same future point in time, it is unclear which of the rates should be regarded as the benchmark rate for discounting a cash flow over the six-month period. Similar difficulties also exist for longer periods. As a result, the first task is to derive a set of unique interest rates for the above time periods, or terms. Such rates are referred to as **implied benchmark spot rates** and they are designated with the notation s_j, where s_j is the spot rate for a term beginning on 6/15/06 and terminating at the end of the *j*th six-month period. Spot rates are "free" of multiple cash flows.

The implied spot rates can be calculated by first examining the six-month issue. Since all the bonds listed in table 5.1 are assumed to pay coupons semiannually, the six-month issue provides only one future cash flow—its principal and interest payment at maturity. Further, since this bond's present value (100), future value (principal + interest = 100 + 3 = 103), and term (0.5 years) are known, there can be only one interest-rate value that relates the three quantities. This value is designated as the implied benchmark six-month spot rate. The value is solved for from the given

EQUATION 5.1

Compound-Interest Equation

$$FV = PV \times (1 + s_j/m)^{(n \times m)}$$

or

$$s_j = m \times \left(\sqrt[(n \times m)]{FV/PV} - 1\right)$$

Where:

FV = Future value

PV = Present value

s_j = Implied benchmark spot rate for period *j* (decimal)

m = Number of compounding periods per year

n = Length of period in years

quantities by using the compound-interest formula, shown as **EQUATION 5.1**.

Equation 5.1 relates a cash flow's present value and future value in terms of an associated interest rate, compounding convention, and time period. Rearranged, it may be used to solve for an implied spot rate. For the six-month benchmark bond, $j = 1$, m = 2, n = 0.5 years, FV = \$103, and PV = \$100. (In this and all calculations throughout the book, end results are determined before rounding intermediate results.)

$$\begin{aligned} s_1 &= 2 \times \left(\sqrt[(0.5 \times 2)]{\$103/\$100} - 1 \right) \\ &= 0.06000 \\ &= 6.000\% \end{aligned}$$

Thus, the implied benchmark six-month spot rate is equal to 6 percent. Next, it is necessary to determine the implied benchmark one-year spot rate for the term from 6/15/06 to 6/15/07. Note that the one-year issue contains two future cash flows: a \$3.50 six-month coupon payment on 12/15/06 and a \$103.50 one-year coupon and principal payment on 6/15/07. Since the first cash flow occurs on 12/15/06—six months from the valuation date—it must be present-valued at the 6 percent benchmark six-month rate established above. Once this present value is determined, it may be subtracted from the \$100 total present value of the one-year issue to obtain the present value of the one-year coupon and principal cash flow. Again, here is a single cash flow with a known present value, future value, and term. The rate that equates these quantities is the implied benchmark one-year spot rate. From equation 5.1, the present value of the six-month \$3.50 coupon payment of the one-year benchmark issue, discounted at the implied six-month spot rate, is:

$$\begin{aligned} PV_{\text{6-mo cash flow, 1-yr bond}} &= \$3.50 \,/\, (1 + 0.06/2)^{(0.5 \times 2)} \\ &= \$3.3981 \end{aligned}$$

The present value of the one-year \$103.50 coupon and principal payment is found by subtracting the present value of the six-month cash flow, determined above, from the total present value of the issue:

$$PV_{\text{1-yr cash flow, 1-yr bond}} = \$100 - \$3.3981$$
$$= \$96.6019$$

The implied benchmark one-year spot rate is then determined by using the \$96.6019 present value of the one-year cash flow determined above:

$$s_2 = 2 \times \left(\sqrt[(1 \times 2)]{\$103.50/\$96.6019} - 1\right)$$
$$= 0.07018$$
$$= 7.018\%$$

The implied benchmark 1.5-year spot rate is solved for similarly:

$$PV_{\text{6-mo cash flow, 1.5-yr bond}} = \$4.00 / (1 + 0.06/2)^{(0.5 \times 2)}$$
$$= \$3.8835$$

$$PV_{\text{1-yr cash flow, 1.5-yr bond}} = \$4.00 / (1 + 0.07018/2)^{(1 \times 2)}$$
$$= \$3.7334$$

$$PV_{\text{1.5-yr cash flow, 1.5-yr bond}} = \$100 - \$3.8835 - \$3.7334$$
$$= \$92.3831$$

$$s_3 = 2 \times \left(\sqrt[(1.5 \times 2)]{\$104/\$92.3831} - 1\right)$$
$$= 0.08054$$
$$= 8.054\%$$

Similar steps give s_4, the implied two-year benchmark spot rate, as 9.117 percent.

Rates s_1, s_2, s_3, and s_4 uniquely describe the benchmark rates for the 6-month, 1-, 1.5-, and 2-year terms that begin on 6/15/06 and end on 12/15/06, 6/15/07, 12/15/07, and 6/15/08, respectively. Note that the 1, 1.5-, and 2-year implied spot rates are progressively greater than the yields for these terms. This phenomenon occurs whenever the yield curve is positively sloped, because the present values of an issue's shorter cash flows are discounted at rates that are lower than its yield. This generates higher present values that, when subtracted from the price of the bond, produce a lower present value for the final cash flow. The lower present value implies a spot rate that is greater than the issue's yield. Negatively sloped curves generate the opposite effect. Precisely flat yield curves generate spot rates equal to the curve's yield.

IN ORDER TO PROJECT a bond's price onto a future date, the binomial-tree model breaks the future into a sequence of discrete time periods. This example employs semiannual time periods, meaning that the model will break the future into a sequence of six-month periods. The model's objective is to determine prices for the underlying security at the end of each six-month period. In the following discussion, it is assumed (momentarily) that no uncertainty exists regarding the value of interest rates in future time periods as implied by the current yield curve. The inherent uncertainty surrounding future interest rates will be addressed at a later stage.

Before this task can be accomplished, the risk-free rates of return for each of the sequential six-month periods must be determined. Now that the set of implied benchmark rates that uniquely describe the rates of return for the 6-month, 1-year, 1.5-year, and 2-year *terms* have been established, the rate of return implied by the yield curve can be determined for the sequence of six-month *periods* beginning on 6/15/06, 12/15/06, 6/15/07, and 12/15/07. These period rates are referred to as "implied benchmark j-period-forward six-month rates" and are designated f_j, where f_j is the implied forward six-month rate for the jth period.

Since the implied benchmark six-month spot rate describes returns for a term that coincides precisely with the first of the series of six-month periods, this rate describes the risk-free rate of return for the first six-month period. Thus, $f_1 = s_1 = 6.000$ percent, where f_1 is the risk-free rate for the first six-month period. The risk-free rates for the second, third, and fourth six-month periods, designated f_2, f_3, and f_4, respectively, are solved for from the implied spot rates.

The benchmark rate for the second semiannual period, f_2, is referred to as the one-period-forward six-month rate, because it goes into effect one six-month period from now ("one-period-forward") and remains in effect for six months ("six-month rate"). This rate, in conjunction with the rate from the first period, f_1, must provide returns that match those generated by the implied one-year spot rate for the entire one-year term. In other words, a dollar invested from 6/15/06 to 12/15/06 at the first period's benchmark rate of 6 percent and then reinvested from 12/15/06 to 6/15/07 at the second period's (as yet unknown) implied forward rate must enjoy the same returns as a dollar invested from 6/15/06 to 6/15/07 at the implied one-year spot rate.

If this equivalency were ignored, an interest-rate environment would be modeled in which the return over a given term would depend on whether an investment were made at one time for the entire term or over a succession of periods within the term. Discrepancies between the two create unrealistic arbitrage conditions: a position for a given term carrying a lower return may be sold short against the simultaneous purchase of a position for the same term carrying a higher return, generating a risk-free, cost-free profit. Period rates must therefore be determined so that they are arbitrage-free.

The rate for the second six-month period—the one-period-forward six-month rate—is determined by computing the future value, at the end of the first six-month period, of \$1 invested at f_1, the first period's benchmark rate:

$$
\begin{aligned}
FV_1 &= \$1 \times (1 + f_1/2)^{(0.5 \times 2)} \\
&= \$1 \times (1 + 0.06/2)^1 \\
&= \$1.0300
\end{aligned}
$$

The future value, at the end of the one-year term, of \$1 invested at the implied benchmark one-year spot rate is determined as follows:

$$\begin{aligned} FV_2 &= \$1 \times (1 + s_2/2)^{(1 \times 2)} \\ &= \$1 \times (1 + 0.07018/2)^2 \\ &= \$1.0714 \end{aligned}$$

The implied benchmark one-period-forward rate, f_2, is the rate that equates the value of FV_1 (\$1.0300) on 12/15/06 to FV_2 (\$1.0714) on 6/15/07. So, from equation 5.1:

$$\begin{aligned} f_2 &= 2 \times (\sqrt[(0.5 \times 2)]{FV_2/FV_1} - 1) \\ &= 2 \times (\$1.0714/\$1.03 - 1) \\ &= 0.08040 \\ &= 8.040\% \end{aligned}$$

In other words, \$1 invested from 6/15/06 to 12/15/06 at 6.000 percent (the implied forward rate for the first period), and then reinvested from 12/15/06 to 6/15/07 at 8.040 percent (the implied forward rate for the second period), would accumulate the same returns as \$1 invested from 6/15/06 to 6/15/07 at 7.018 percent (the implied one-year spot rate).

The rate for the third six-month period—the two-period-forward six-month rate—is determined in a similar way:

$$\begin{aligned} FV_3 &= \$1 \times (1 + s_3/2)^{(1.5 \times 2)} \\ &= \$1 \times (1 + 0.08054/2)^3 \\ &= \$1.1257 \end{aligned}$$

$$\begin{aligned} f_3 &= 2 \times (\sqrt[(0.5 \times 2)]{FV_3/FV_2} - 1) \\ &= 2 \times (\$1.1257/\$1.0714 - 1) \\ &= 0.10144 \\ &= 10.144\% \end{aligned}$$

Finally, f_4, the three-period-forward six-month rate, is similarly calculated as 12.338 percent.

The results of the implied spot- and forward-rate calculations, along with the given yield curve, are displayed in **TABLE 5.2**. The

TABLE 5.2

Benchmark Yields, Implied Spot Rates, and Implied Forward Rates

Years to Maturity	Observed Benchmark Yield	Implied Benchmark Spot Rate	Implied Benchmark Forward 6-Month Rate
0.5	6.000%	6.000%	6.000%
1.0	7.000%	7.018%	8.040%
1.5	8.000%	8.054%	10.144%
2.0	9.000%	9.117%	12.338%

results provide a set of reference rates that can be used to consistently value any set of cash flows through a path of possible outcomes.

CHAPTER 6

BEYOND THE LOGNORMAL MODEL

THOUGH OPTION-ADJUSTED SPREAD (OAS) analysis provides a marked improvement over conventional yield analysis for measuring the risk and return of nonbullet bonds, its results and sophistication depend on the particular interest-rate option model employed in the analysis. The model described in the preceding chapters—known in technical terminology as a "one-factor, arbitrage-free, binomial tree of lognormally distributed **short rates**"—is usually referred to simply as the "lognormal model."

One distinguishing feature of this model is its use of a single **volatility** input. This single volatility essentially assumes that the rate at which interest rates change is the same for all maturities along the yield curve. This assumption is at odds with empirical evidence, which shows that the volatility of short-term interest rates significantly exceeds that of long-term interest rates. In an effort to compensate for this limitation, many users of lognormal models tend to specify high volatility assumptions on short-term bonds and low volatilities on long-term bonds. However, since different volatility assumptions cause the model to create different interest-rate environments, dissimilar bonds analyzed in this manner will not have comparable results. Thus, in such circumstances, the lognormal model may force users to choose between a consistent interest-rate model and a realistic one.

To address this shortcoming, modelers have developed interest-rate option processes that utilize a **term structure of volatility (TSOV)**. These so-called TSOV models extend the precision of lognormal models by allowing users to specify a volatility curve whose values vary with maturity. Because such an analysis can easily incorporate the attenuated volatilities of long-term interest rates, a consistent interest-rate process can be applied to bonds with widely varying maturities and option expirations, resulting in realistically derived, comparable OAS risk and return values. The chief obstacle to using the TSOV model is the difficulty of specifying an accurate **volatility curve**.

In addition to an inverted volatility curve, empirical data also suggest that interest rates tend toward mean reversion. This means that when interest rates undergo large displacements from historically "normal" levels, strong forces are exerted to push them back toward the norm. The benefit of incorporating this property into an interest-rate model is that it allows the user to control the extent to which rates inhabit abnormally high or low levels and so generate a more reasonable measure of OAS and option value. This is accomplished by specifying an additional model input called the "mean reversion speed," which is usually the inverse of the time required for a rate to revert fully to normal levels. A high mean-reversion speed, such as 0.1, forces rates back to normal levels in roughly ten years and prevents models from generating an overabundance of unrealistically high or low interest rates. A low speed, such as 0.04, forces rates back in twenty-five years and introduces less forceful mean reversion.

These (and other) advances in financial modeling are driven by the classic market desire to find and profit from mispriced securities. As the inexorable process of increasing market efficiency leads to narrower spreads, the complexity and sophistication of financial instruments—and the means by which they are analyzed—will grow steadily. Developing an intuitive understanding of the basic tenets of more sophisticated analytical techniques such as OAS analysis, as well as of their limitations, will allow traders, marketers, and investors to evaluate the performance of a wide range of securities confidently. As a result, the techniques are valuable additions to the tools utilized by financial professionals to evaluate individual securities and portfolios alike.

CHAPTER 7

VOLATILITY AND THE BINOMIAL TREE

IN CHAPTER 5, a set of risk-free interest rates for a sequence of future semiannual periods were derived from the observed yields of benchmark bonds that make up the risk-free yield curve. Each implied forward rate quantifies the risk-free rate of return for the six-month period with which it is associated and forms the framework on which the binomial interest-rate tree is built. These implied forward rates, along with their associated periods, are shown in **FIGURE 7.1**.

If option models were simply to use implied forward rates to generate a price for an option's underlying bond on a future date, their analyses would implicitly assume that interest rates implied by today's market for future periods would occur with absolute certainty. Such an approach would essentially duplicate the simplistic approach of yield-to-worst analysis by assuming that interest rates remain unchanged from settlement to a future pricing date. To avoid this error, *the binomial process models interest rates that vary, rather than remain fixed, over time. This is accomplished by treating implied forward rates as outcomes of a binomial process.* Forward rates modeled in this manner are referred to as "short rates."

In a binomial interest-rate process, a binomial tree of possible short rates for each future time period is constructed. Whereas the

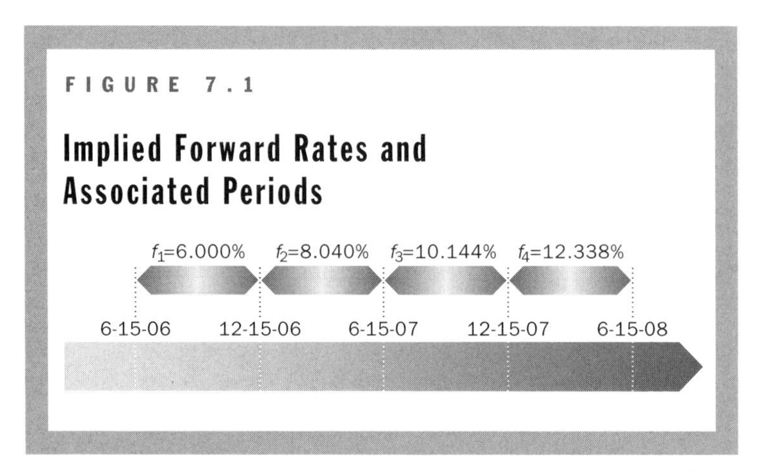

binomial tree for the coin-toss example modeled heads or tails as the two possible outcomes of a given toss, the binomial tree of short interest rates models two interest rates as the possible outcomes of the previous period. A typical binomial interest-rate process is shown in **FIGURE 7.2**.

In this figure, point *A*, hereafter referred to as node *A*, coincides with the start of time period *j*, over which short rate *Rj* is in effect. At the conclusion of period *j*, a new short rate goes into effect for period *j*+1. This may take one of two possible values: $R_{j+1,L}$, the "low" short-rate outcome for period *j*+1, shown at node *B*, or $R_{j+1,H}$, the "high" short-rate outcome, at node *C*. As in the coin-toss example, $R_{j+1,L}$ and $R_{j+1,H}$ are each considered to have a 50 percent chance of occurring and are viewed as the only possible outcomes for period *j*+1's short rate from node *A*.

Modeling interest rates in the manner depicted in figure 7.2 allows the binomial analysis to incorporate the inherent uncertainty associated with quantifying future interest rates. Instead of assuming a single value for a future period's short rate, the model defines a range of possible values for this rate. The range is characterized by the values of the rate's lower and upper boundaries—$R_{j+1,L}$ and $R_{j+1,H}$ in figure 7.2. If the uncertainty associated with a particular period's short rate is high, the rate will have a relatively wide range of possible values and the ratio of the range's upper

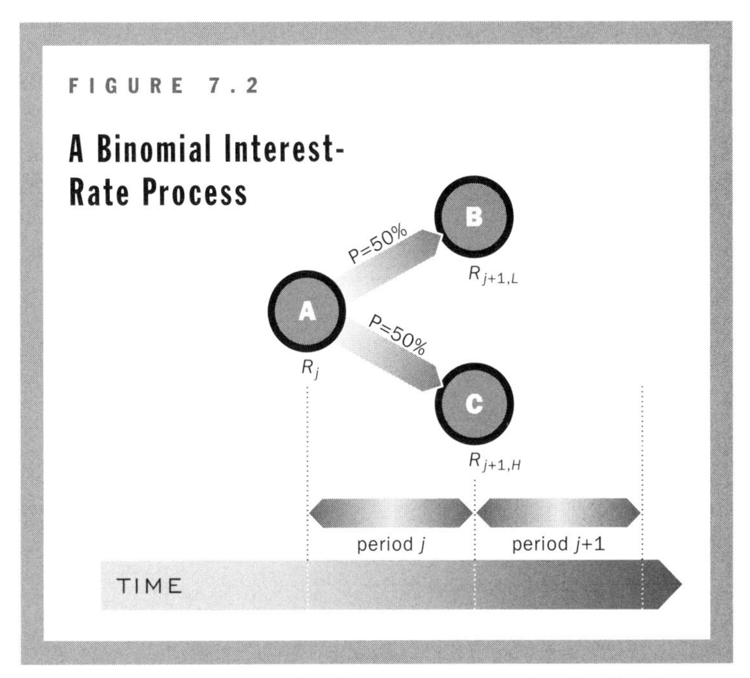

FIGURE 7.2

A Binomial Interest-Rate Process

value to its lower value will be large. In contrast, low levels of uncertainty would imply a relatively narrow range of possible values and a small upper-to-lower-value ratio.

The binomial-tree model allows practitioners to select the level of uncertainty employed in an analysis by specifying the value of an uncertainty parameter, referred to as the **percent volatility of short rates**. Percent volatility can be thought of as the speed at which future short rates change from their current implied values; it is an assumption about the propensity of implied forward rates to change over time. Practitioners often qualify opinions about future volatility by studying two types of quantified uncertainty measures: **historical volatility** and **implied volatility**.

Historical, or empirical, volatility is a statistical measure of a security's past propensity to change value and is determined from historical price or yield data over a specified period. Implied volatility is calculated in an option-valuation model, using the observed prices of options, and gives an indication of the market's view of

EQUATION 7.1

Percent Volatility of a Short Rate *R*

$$V(R) = \frac{(1/\sqrt{\Delta t}) \times \ln(R_H/R_L)}{2}$$

Where:
$V(R)$ = Percent volatility of short rate R
Δt = Length of time period, in years
$\ln(R_H/R_L)$ = Natural logarithm of (R_H/R_L)
R_H = High value of possible outcome of short rate R
R_L = Low value of possible outcome of short rate R

EQUATION 7.2

$$\ln(R_H/R_L) = 2 \times V(R) \times \sqrt{\Delta t}$$

EQUATION 7.3

$$e^{\ln(W)} = \ln(e^W) = W$$

EQUATION 7.4

$$R_H/R_L = e^{\ln(R_H/R_L)} = e^{2 \times V(R) \times \sqrt{\Delta t}}$$

EQUATION 7.5

$$R_H = R_L \times e^{2 \times V(R) \times \sqrt{\Delta t}}$$

the underlying security's future propensity to change value. In general, relatively high volatility levels accompany periods of great uncertainty.

EQUATION 7.1 expresses the percent volatility of a short rate R in terms of given possible high and low outcomes. If, instead, volatility is specified, this equation may be rearranged to solve for R_H and R_L, as shown in **EQUATION 7.2**. This relationship is one of the fundamental building blocks of the lognormal binomial model.

The irrational number *e*, which is roughly equal to 2.7182818, forms the base of the natural logarithms. The relationship between *e*, a number *W*, and its natural logarithm is shown in **EQUATION 7.3**.

Applying the relationship shown in equation 7.3 to equation 7.2 allows us to restate equation 7.2 as **EQUATION 7.4**. A slight rearrangement of equation 7.4 gives **EQUATION 7.5**.

Equation 7.4 states that the ratio of the high short-rate outcome to the low short-rate outcome is equal to the base of the natural logarithms raised to a power of twice the volatility rate times the square root of the time interval. High volatility levels, specified to reflect relatively high levels of interest-rate uncertainty, will increase the term $e^{2 \times V(R) \times \sqrt{\Delta t}}$ and bring about a relatively large value for the R_H/R_L ratio. This is consistent with the logic formulated earlier, in which greater uncertainty led to a larger ratio of upper-to-lower possible short rates. Low volatility specifications will cause the term $e^{2 \times V(R) \times \sqrt{\Delta t}}$ to take on a lower value, thereby decreasing the value of the R_H/R_L ratio.

Equation 7.5 states that the high short-rate outcome, R_H, is proportional to the low short-rate outcome, R_L, where the proportionality factor is the term $e^{2 \times V(R) \times \sqrt{\Delta t}}$. In this case, a high volatility assumption will increase the magnitude of this proportionality factor and generate a relatively high value for R_H. For the same R_L and Δt, a low volatility assumption will generate a lower value for R_H. One of the key advantages of using such a proportionality factor for building an interest-rate model is that it prevents the creation of negative interest rates, a feature not shared by some other option models.

In either of the equations 7.4 or 7.5, a high volatility level will translate into a wider range of possible values for a given period's short rate. Once again, the consistency of the relationship between a high degree of uncertainty and a high volatility level is visible.

As an example, recall that the OAS model divides the future into a series of six-month time periods, giving $\Delta t = 0.5$ years. At a volatility of 10 percent, $V(R) = 0.10$, and equation 7.5 gives:

$$R_H = R_L \times e^{2 \times V(R) \times \sqrt{\Delta t}}$$
$$= R_L \times 2.7182818^{2 \times .10 \times \sqrt{0.50}}$$
$$= R_L \times 1.15191$$

At a volatility of 10 percent, the high short-rate outcome is roughly 1.15 times greater than the low short-rate outcome. If a higher volatility of 20 percent is specified, a higher proportionality factor is generated:

$$R_H = R_L \times e^{2 \times V(R) \times \sqrt{\Delta t}}$$
$$= R_L \times 2.7182818^{2 \times 0.20 \times \sqrt{0.50}}$$
$$= R_L \times 1.326896$$

At the higher volatility rate of 0.20, the high short-rate outcome is roughly 1.33 times greater than the low short-rate outcome.

The above relationships and calculations provide information about the magnitude of a particular short rate only in terms of an adjacent short rate. To determine the actual values of the short rates in the binomial tree, it is necessary to first establish their approximate values using the implied forward rates solved for in Chapter 5. It is crucial to note that these are merely approximations and, if used as is, would produce an incorrect analysis. In Chapter 8, these rates will be fine-tuned to arrive at the correct values.

FIGURE 7.3 shows the binomial tree of risk-free short rates based on the yield curve presented in Chapter 5, its implied forward rates, and an **assumed volatility** rate of 10 percent per year. For the first six-month period, from 6/15/06 to 12/15/06, the risk-free rate, designated as $f_{1,A}$, is 6.000 percent. The designation signifies that the rate $f_{1,A}$ occurs in period 1 at node *A*. Because this rate is associated with a six-month period that begins immediately (on 6/15/06) and is immediately available from the six-month benchmark issue, its value is absolutely certain. As a result, 6.000 percent is the only possible risk-free rate for the first six-month period, as shown at node *A*.

From node *A*, the binomial process dictates that the value of the short rate for the second six-month period must have two

FIGURE 7.3

Binomial Tree of Risk-Free Short Rates

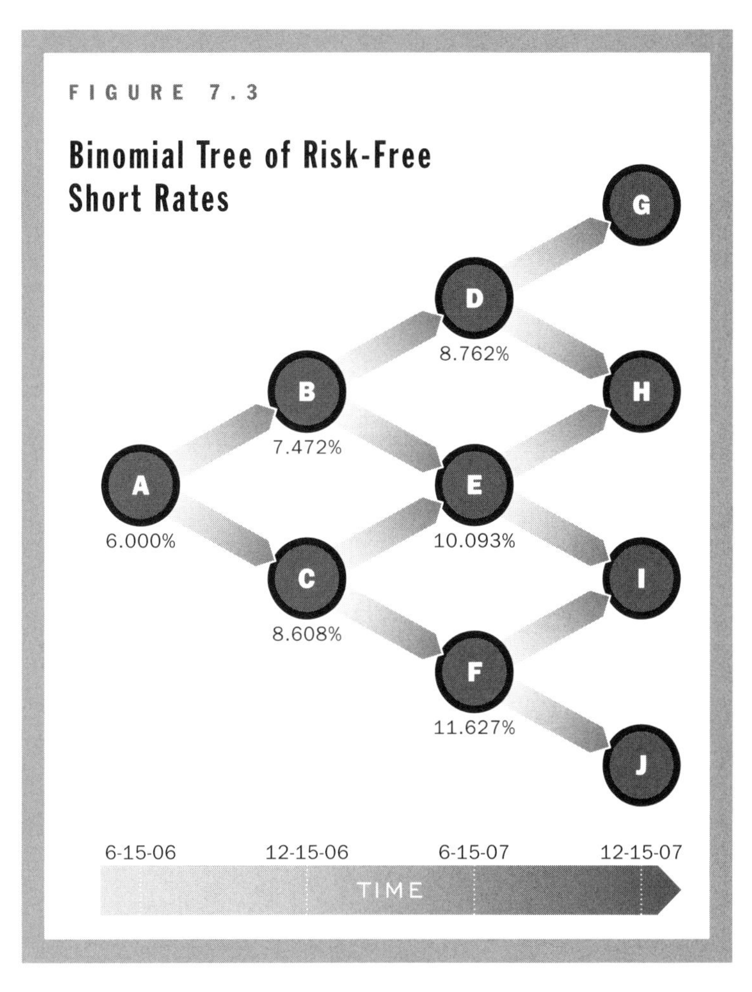

possible values. These values are shown at nodes B and C on 12/15/06, the start of the second six-month period. The rates at these nodes, $f_{2,B}$ and $f_{2,C}$, describe the two possible values that f_2, the risk-free rate for the second period, may carry. To determine these values, two conditions are used: First, equation 7.4 or 7.5 is used to govern the ratio of the adjacent rates at nodes B and C. Second, equation 4.1 is used to constrain the expected value of the two rates to provide the same return as the implied forward rate for the second six-month period. As with the coin toss, both rates have equal chances of occurring. These conditions are stated below algebraically.

$$\text{Condition 1: } f_{2,C}/f_{2,B} = 1.15191,$$

or

$$f_{2,C} = f_{2,B} \times 1.15191$$

$$\text{Condition 2: } (f_{2,C} \times 0.50) + (f_{2,B} \times 0.50) = 8.040\%$$

Substituting the expression for $f_{2,C}$ from Condition 1 into Condition 2 gives:

$$[(f_{2,B} \times 1.15191) \times 0.50] + (f_{2,B} \times 0.50) = 8.040\%$$

or

$$f_{2,B} = 7.472\%$$

Substituting this value for $f_{2,B}$ in Condition 1 and solving for $f_{2,C}$ gives:

$$\begin{aligned} f_{2,C} &= 7.472\% \times 1.15191 \\ &= 8.608\% \end{aligned}$$

Thus, in period two, the risk-free short rate f_2 may have two possible values: 7.472 percent at node *B* and 8.608 percent at node *C*. From each of these two nodes, the binomial process dictates that two possible values exist as outcomes for the short rate in the next (third) six-month period. Once again, the ratio of the values of adjacent rates in this period is determined by the volatility rate, and the expected value of all possible short rates for the period must provide the same return as the implied forward rate for the third six-month period.

For the third period, three conditions exist: The first pertains to the ratio of short rates at nodes *D* and *E*, the second pertains to the ratio of short rates at nodes *E* and *F*, and the third pertains to the expected value of the rates at nodes *D*, *E*, and *F* in relation to the implied forward rate for the period. Conditions 1 and 2 are stated below.

$$\text{Condition 1: } f_{3,E}/f_{3,D} = 1.15191,$$

or

$$f_{3,E} = f_{3,D} \times 1.15191$$

$$\text{Condition 2: } f_{3,F}/f_{3,E} = 1.15191,$$

or

$$f_{3,F} = f_{3,E} \times 1.15191$$
$$= (f_{3,D} \times 1.15191) \times 1.15191$$

In order to formulate Condition 3, the probabilities associated with the rates at nodes *D*, *E*, and *F* must be established. This is accomplished by noting that, from node *A*, only one path (*ABD*) arrives at node *D*, only one path (*ACF*) arrives at node *F*, and two paths (*ABE* and *ACE*) arrive at node *E*. In other words, from node *A*, there is a one-in-four, or 25 percent, chance of arriving at node *D*, a 25 percent chance of arriving at node *F*, and a two-in-four, or 50 percent, chance of arriving at node *E*. Accordingly, Condition 3 is stated below.

$$\text{Condition 3: } (f_{3,D} \times 0.25) + (f_{3,E} \times 0.50) + (f_{3,F} \times 0.25) = 10.144\%$$

Substituting the expressions for $f_{3,E}$ and $f_{3,F}$ from Conditions 1 and 2, respectively, into Condition 3 gives:

$$(f_{3,D} \times 0.25) + [(f_{3,D} \times 1.15191) \times 0.50] + \{[f_{3,D} \times (1.15191)2] \times 0.25\}$$
$$= 10.144\%,$$

or

$$f_{3,D} \times \{0.25 + (1.15191 \times 0.50) + [(1.15191)2 \times 0.25]\}$$
$$= 10.144\%$$

or

$$f_{3,D} = 8.762\%$$

Substituting this value into Conditions 1 and 2 gives:

$$f_{3,E} = 8.762\% \times 1.15191$$
$$= 10.093\%$$
$$f_{3,F} = 8.762\% \times (1.15191)^2$$
$$= 11.627\%$$

The preceding calculations show that f_3, period three's short rate, has three possible values: 8.762 percent at node *D*, 10.093 percent at node *E*, and 11.627 percent at node *F*. Rates for the next period, if required, are derived in a similar manner. Each of period three's short rates would have two possible outcomes for the fourth period, giving rise to four possible values for f_4. These values would be shown at nodes *G*, *H*, *I*, and *J*. Short rates for subsequent periods may be generated in a similar manner, with each successive period increasing by one its number of possible rates.

With the construction of the binomial tree of risk-free short rates completed, the next task is to verify that the rates it contains do not introduce any bias into the returns it models. This subject will be addressed in Chapter 8.

CHAPTER 8

MATCHING THE MODEL TO THE MARKET

CHAPTER 7 STATED that the *expected value of the short rates in a given period must provide the same return as the implied forward rate for that period.* Although this condition seemed logical and helped estimate the short rates that appeared in the binomial tree, it provides only a first approximation of their values. In reality, it is far more important for the binomial tree to generate a model-predicted price for a benchmark bond that matches its observed price in the market. This requirement is perhaps the most crucial—and delicate—aspect of constructing such a model.

To test the suitability of the short rates calculated in Chapter 7, the binomial tree will be used to generate a model-predicted price for one of the benchmark bonds shown in table 5.1, in which the hypothetical yield curve for 6/15/06 is described. To this end, all computed prices in this chapter will be displayed to the fourth, rather than the second, decimal place.

If the model generates a price for a chosen benchmark bond that matches its observed price, the rates in the tree may be considered appropriate and the construction of the model sound. On the other hand, a model price that differs from an observed price indicates that the short rates must be calibrated until the proper price is generated.

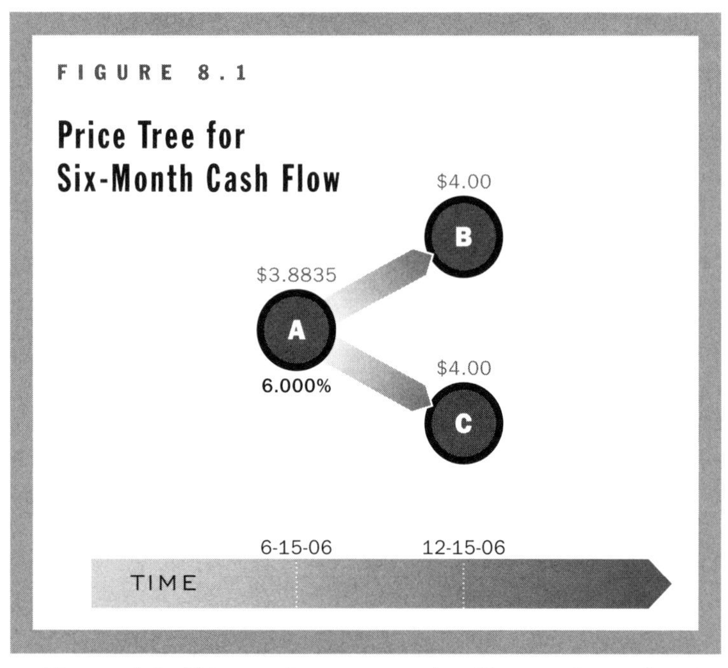

The model will be used as an example of how to determine the price for the 1.5-year benchmark bond. This issue carries an 8 percent coupon and matures on 12/15/07, precisely 1.5 years from the 6/15/06 settlement date. A $100 face amount of this issue provides three future cash flows: a $4.00 6-month coupon payment on 12/15/06, a $4.00 1-year coupon payment on 6/15/07, and a $104.00 1.5-year coupon and principal payment on 12/15/07. The market price of this bond—which represents the present value of these three future cash flows—is observed to be $100 on 6/15/06. If the binomial tree is constructed properly, the short rates it contains should generate a model price of $100.

A model-predicted price for this issue is generated by determining the present value, on 6/15/06, of each of the three future cash flows. On 12/15/06, the six-month coupon payment date, the value of this payment will be precisely $4.00, regardless of the level of interest rates on that date. Accordingly, this value is shown at nodes *B* and *C* in **FIGURE 8.1**, the price tree for the six-month cash flow. In order to determine the present value of this cash flow, its expected future value must be discounted over the six-month period between its 12/15/06 payment date and the 6/15/06 settlement date. The discount rate is the short rate associated with the node to which the cash flow is to be discounted—node *A* in this case. As has already been established, the rate at this node, $f_{1,A}$, is 6.000 percent.

The expected value of this cash flow on 12/15/06 is determined by weighting each possible price outcome, shown at nodes *B* and *C*, by the probability that it will occur. Since both outcomes are assumed to have equal chances of occurring, a probability of 50 percent is associated with each of the prices at nodes *B* and *C*:

$$
\begin{aligned}
P_{\text{expected}} &= (P_B \times 0.50) + (P_C \times 0.50) \\
&= \frac{P_B + P_C}{2}
\end{aligned}
$$

The present value is found by discounting the expected value of the cash flow over the intervening period at the appropriate risk-free short rate. This is accomplished using equation 5.1, the compound interest formula, which is restated in **EQUATION 8.1** to solve for a present value given a general annualized interest rate *r*.

EQUATION 8.1

Compound-Interest Equation

$$PV = FV/[(1 + r/m)^{(n \times m)}]$$

Where:

PV = Present value

FV = Future value

r = Annualized interest rate (decimal)

m = Number of compounding periods per year

n = Length of period in years

EQUATION 8.2

Binomial-Tree Price Equation

$$P_{j,i} = \frac{(P_{j+1,i+1} + P_{j+1,i})}{2} \times \frac{1}{(1 + \frac{f_{j,i}}{2})}$$

Where:

$P_{j,i}$ = Price of cash flow on date *j*, at node *i*

$P_{j+1,i+1}$ = Price of cash flow one period in the future from date *j*, on date *j*+1, at node *i*+1

$P_{j+1,i}$ = Price of cash flow on date *j*+1, at node *i*

$f_{j,i}$ = Short rate for period commencing on date *j*, at node *i* (decimal)

In this example, FV = $P_{expected}$, $r = f_{1,A}$, m = 2 (semiannual compounding), and n = 0.5 (length of the first six-month period, in years). Substituting these values into equation 8.1 gives:

$$PV_{1,A} = P_{expected}/[(1 + f_{1,A}/2)^{0.5 \times 2}],$$

or

$$PV_{1,A} = \frac{P_{2,B} + P_{2,C}}{2} / (1 + f_{1,A}/2)$$

Since all the short rates in the tree are annualized rates that assume semiannual compounding and each of the periods is six months in length, the above expression may be generalized to apply to any node in the tree. This generalized form is shown as **EQUATION 8.2**.

In this case, $P_{j+1,i+1} = P_{2,B} =$ \$4.00, $P_{j+1,i} = P_{2,C} =$ \$4.00, $f_{j,i} = f_{1,A} =$ 6.000%, and it follows to solve for $P_{j,i} = P_{1,A}$. Substituting these values into equation 8.2 gives:

$$P_{1,A\text{ six-month cash flow}} = \frac{(\$4.00 + \$4.00)}{2} \times \frac{1}{(1 + \frac{0.0600}{2})}$$

$$= \$3.8835$$

Thus, the model generates a 6/15/06 value of $3.8835 for the six-month cash flow, as shown in figure 8.1.

We next turn to the one-year cash flow, the price tree for which is shown in **FIGURE 8.2**. On 6/15/07, the one-year coupon payment date, this cash flow has a value of $4.00, shown at nodes *D*, *E*, and *F*. In order to determine the value of this cash flow at node *A*, its value must first be determined at nodes *B* and *C*. The value at node *B* is found by using equation 8.2:

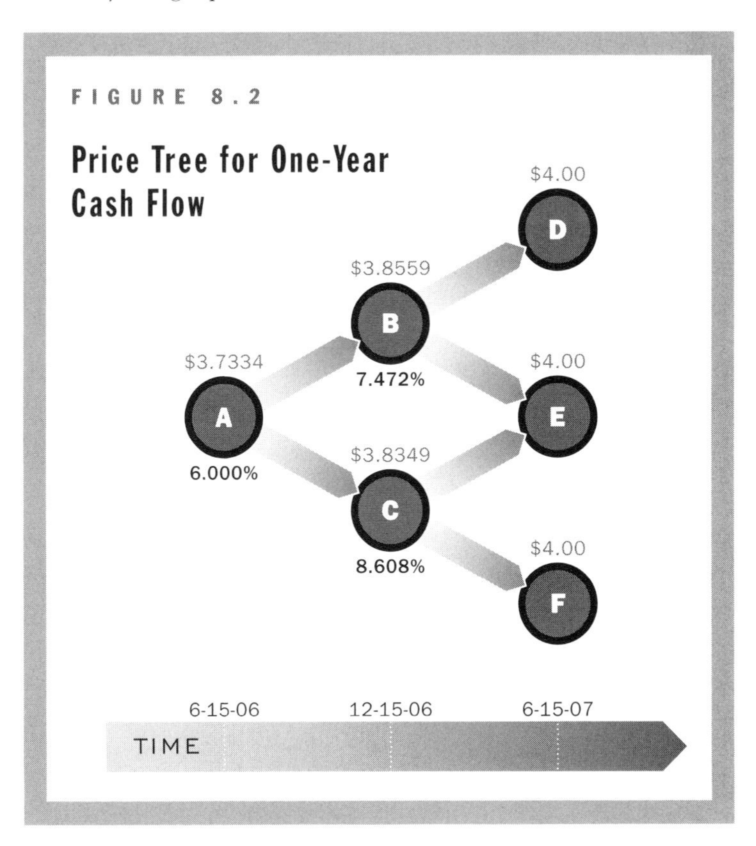

$$P_{2,B\text{ one-year cash flow}} = \frac{(P_{3,D} + P_{3,E})}{2} \times \frac{1}{(1 + \frac{f_{2,B}}{2})}$$

$$= \frac{(\$4.00 + \$4.00)}{2} \times \frac{1}{(1 + \frac{0.07472}{2})}$$

$$= \$3.8559$$

The value at node *C* is found similarly:

$$P_{2,C\text{ one-year cash flow}} = \frac{(P_{3,E} + P_{3,F})}{2} \times \frac{1}{(1 + \frac{f_{2,C}}{2})}$$

$$= \frac{(\$4.00 + \$4.00)}{2} \times \frac{1}{(1 + \frac{0.08608}{2})}$$

$$= \$3.8349$$

The value at node *A* is found by present-valuing the cash flow's expected value on 12/15/06, using the prices at nodes *B* and *C*:

$$P_{1,A\text{ one-year cash flow}} = \frac{(P_{2,B} + P_{2,C})}{2} \times \frac{1}{(1 + \frac{f_{1,A}}{2})}$$

$$= \frac{(\$3.8559 + \$3.8349)}{2} \times \frac{1}{(1 + \frac{0.06000}{2})}$$

$$= \$3.7334$$

Thus, the model generates a 6/15/06 value of $3.7334 for the one-year cash flow.

Lastly, the 6/15/06 value of the 1.5-year cash flow must be determined. **FIGURE 8.3** contains the price tree for this cash flow. Price calculations are shown below:

$$P_{4,G} = P_{4,H} = P_{4,I} = P_{4,J} = \$104.00$$

The model generates three 6/15/07 values for this cash flow:

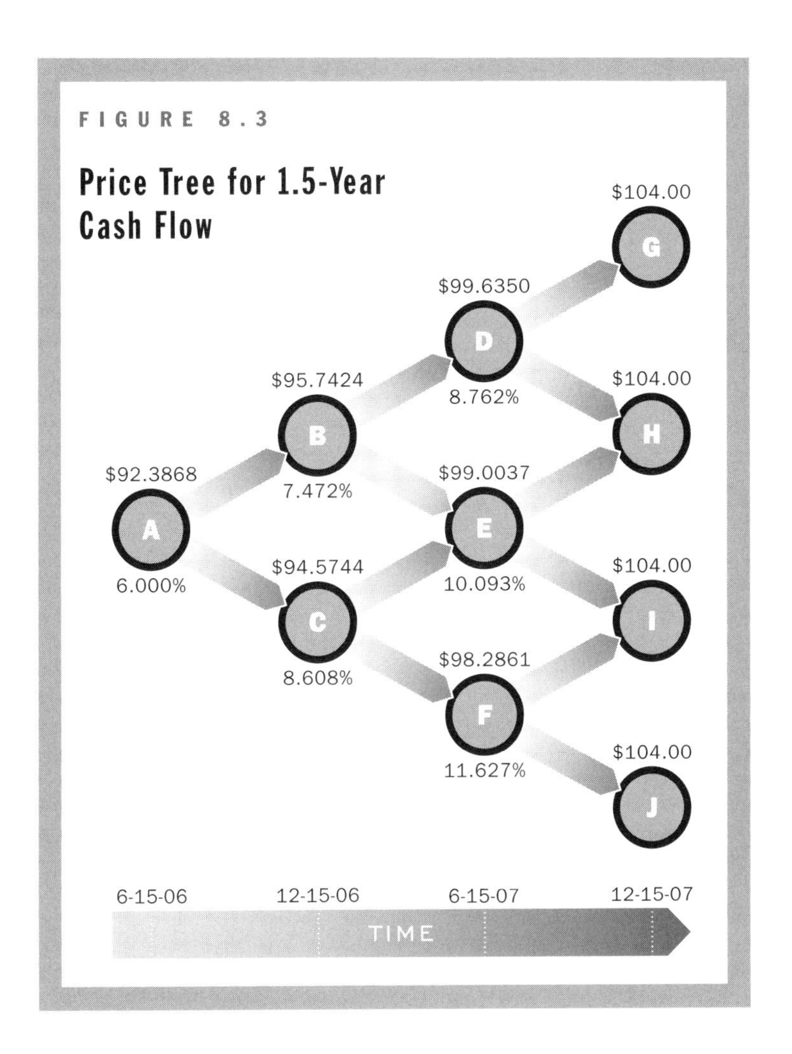

$$P_{3,D\ \text{1.5-year cash flow}} = \frac{(P_{4,G} + P_{4,H})}{2} \times \frac{1}{(1 + \frac{f_{3,D}}{2})}$$

$$= \frac{(\$104.00 + \$104.00)}{2} \times \frac{1}{(1 + \frac{0.08762}{2})}$$

$$= \$99.6350$$

$$P_{3,E\ 1.5\text{-year cash flow}} = \frac{(P_{4,H} + P_{4,I})}{2} \times \frac{1}{(1 + \frac{f_{3,E}}{2})}$$

$$= \frac{(\$104.00 + \$104.00)}{2} \times \frac{1}{(1 + \frac{0.10093}{2})}$$

$$= \$99.0037$$

$$P_{3,F\ 1.5\text{-year cash flow}} = \frac{(P_{4,I} + P_{4,J})}{2} \times \frac{1}{(1 + \frac{f_{3,F}}{2})}$$

$$= \frac{(\$104.00 + \$104.00)}{2} \times \frac{1}{(1 + \frac{0.11627}{2})}$$

$$= \$98.2861$$

From the above calculations, two possible prices are modeled for 12/15/06:

$$P_{2,B\ 1.5\text{-year cash flow}} = \frac{(P_{3,D} + P_{3,E})}{2} \times \frac{1}{(1 + \frac{f_{2,B}}{2})}$$

$$= \frac{(\$99.6350 + \$99.0037)}{2} \times \frac{1}{(1 + \frac{0.07472}{2})}$$

$$= \$95.7424$$

$$P_{2,C\ 1.5\text{-year cash flow}} = \frac{(P_{3,E} + P_{3,F})}{2} \times \frac{1}{(1 + \frac{f_{2,C}}{2})}$$

$$= \frac{(\$99.0037 + \$98.2861)}{2} \times \frac{1}{(1 + \frac{0.08608}{2})}$$

$$= \$94.5744$$

The value at node *A* is determined using the above values:

$$P_{1,A\ 1.5\text{-year cash flow}} = \frac{(P_{2,B} + P_{2,C})}{2} \times \frac{1}{(1 + \frac{f_{1,A}}{2})}$$

$$= \frac{(\$95.7424 + \$94.5744)}{2} \times \frac{1}{(1 + \frac{0.06000}{2})}$$

$$= \$92.3868$$

Now that the model-predicted present value of the 6-month, 1-year, and 1.5-year cash flows are determined, compute the model-predicted price for the bond as their sum:

$$P_{\text{model-predicted}} = \$3.8835 + \$3.7334 + \$92.3868$$
$$= \$100.0037$$

Although the difference between the \$100.0037 model-predicted price and the \$100 observed market price is small, it nonetheless indicates that the rates in the tree do not generate the observed price of a bond. If the tree were constructed to incorporate a greater number of future periods, the discrepancy between observed and model-generated values would be larger.

To overcome this flaw, the rates in the binomial tree must be calibrated so that they generate prices that match observed values. This is done by making successive estimates of a single period rate, using the volatility ratio to establish the values of other possible rates for the period, and repeating the pricing procedure detailed above until the estimated rates generate the desired price. Although a seemingly daunting task, efficient computer-run routines are able to converge on the appropriate rate values very rapidly. The results of such a trial-and-error process are shown as the calibrated binomial tree in **FIGURE 8.4**, which contains short rates for the first three six-month periods. It is this tree that will form the basis of the OAS analysis.

The model-generated price's drift away from the bond's observed price is a consequence of the volatility rate specified for the analysis. The volatility parameter manifests itself as a component of the proportionality factor between adjacent short rates in

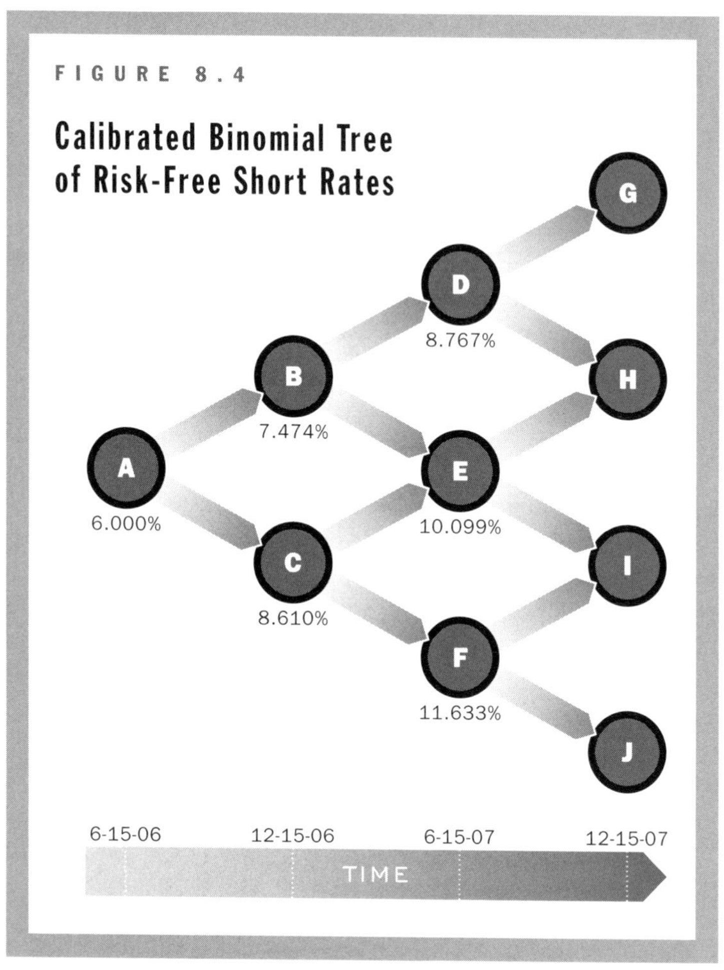

a given period. Although the ratio between adjacent short rates is constant, the absolute difference between the rates decreases as their values decline. For example, in the uncalibrated tree, period three has three possible short rates: 11.627, 10.093, and 8.762 percent. In this series, the ratio of one rate to the next is constant, but the difference between their values declines as the rates decrease: 11.627 – 10.093 = 153.4 basis points, whereas 10.093 – 8.762 = 133.1 basis points. The smaller differences between the lower rates have the effect of weighting the lower rates—and their corresponding higher prices—more heavily in a given period. As a result, the modeled value of a cash flow is higher than its observed value. This is why the model-generated price was greater than the observed price of the bond, and why the calibrated tree contains rates that are slightly higher than those calculated in Chapter 7. In addition, the greater the specified volatility rate, the more pronounced this effect and the greater the price drift introduced by the model. Another important aspect of the lognormal volatility parameter is that, for a given volatility level, the absolute range of rates for a period increases as the underlying rate level increases.

The effect of overemphasizing the lower rates can be seen by comparing the uncalibrated model-predicted present value of one of the bond's cash flows with its implied-forward-rate-predicted value. Since the rates for a given period were originally determined so that their expected value equaled the implied forward rate for the period, the two prices are expected to match. However, this is not the case.

Consider the \$92.3868 uncalibrated model-predicted value of the 1.5-year cash flow of the 1.5-year bond. The implied forward rates for periods one, two, and three, solved for in Chapter 5 and shown in figure 7.1, are 6.000, 8.040, and 10.144 percent, respectively. The present value of this cash flow, as determined by these implied forward rates, is found by discounting its \$104.00 redemption value over each successive period at the appropriate rate. This is shown below:

$$P_{6/15/07} = \frac{P_{12/15/07}}{(1 + \frac{f3}{2})}$$

$$P_{12/15/06} = \frac{P_{6/15/07}}{(1 + \frac{f2}{2})} = \frac{P_{12/15/07}}{(1 + \frac{f3}{2})} \times \frac{1}{(1 + \frac{f2}{2})}$$

$$P_{6/15/06} = P_{12/15/06} = P_{12/15/07} \times \frac{1}{(1 + \frac{f1}{2})(1 + \frac{f3}{2}) \times (1 + \frac{f2}{2})(1 + \frac{f1}{2})}$$

or

$$P_{6/15/06} = \frac{P_{12/15/07}}{(1 + \frac{f_1}{2}) \times (1 + \frac{f_2}{2}) \times (1 + \frac{f_3}{2})}$$

Substituting gives:

$$P_{6/15/06} = \frac{\$104.00}{(1 + \frac{0.06000}{2}) \times (1 + \frac{0.08040}{2}) \times (1 + \frac{0.10144}{2})}$$

$$= \$92.3831$$

Even though each period in the uncalibrated model has an expected rate of return that equals the implied forward rate for the period, the cash flow's actual value of $92.3831 is overestimated by the model as $92.3868, a difference of $0.0037 per $100 face value. Since the model's price overestimation occurs for each of a bond's cash flows, the magnitude of the upward price drift increases as the number of cash flows provided by the bond increases.

For the special case in which a volatility rate of zero is specified, equation 7.4 gives the following result:

$$R_H/R_L = e^{(2 \times 0.00 \times \sqrt{0.50})} = e^0 = 1,$$

or

$$R_H = R_L$$

Thus, assuming a volatility of zero causes all the short rates in a given period to have the same value, in effect collapsing the two-dimensional binomial tree into a one-dimensional line. In this case, the value of each period's short rate simply equals the implied forward rate for the period. In other words, zero volatility means that the actual values that interest rates will have in the future are predicted with absolute certainty by their current implied values. This is completely consistent with the earlier interpretation of uncertainty, since zero volatility implies an absence of uncertainty for a given short rate's value.

Although an uncalibrated model generates accurate prices for cash flows under zero-volatility conditions, it does not provide the benefit derived from considering multiple interest-rate scenarios. So, this approach would have the same disadvantages as yield-to-worst calculations for callable bonds.

PART FOUR

Measuring the Spread

CHAPTER 9

BULLET BONDS

UP TO NOW, the focus has been on the construction and calibration of the binomial tree of risk-free short rates. With these tasks completed, the next step is to employ the model to evaluate the return of a bond. This chapter examines the simple case of a non-benchmark bullet bond and develops the notion of spread within the context of the binomial tree. In Chapter 10, the inquiry will extend to the more complex case of a bond containing an embedded option.

The binomial model evaluates the return of a bond by measuring the extent to which its return exceeds the returns described by the risk-free short rates in the tree. The difference between these returns is expressed as a spread and is viewed as the incremental return of a bond at a given price. The determination of the spread involves the following steps. First, the binomial tree is used to generate a model-predicted price for a given bond. Second, the model-predicted price is compared with the bond's observed price. Third, if the two prices differ, the rates in the binomial tree are altered by some uniform amount, the spread estimate. Fourth, using the altered rates, a new model-predicted price is generated and compared with the observed price. Steps three and four are repeated until the model-predicted price matches the bond's observed price.

FIGURE 9.1

Price Tree for Six-Month Coupon Payment of VSB Bond Using Risk-Free Rates

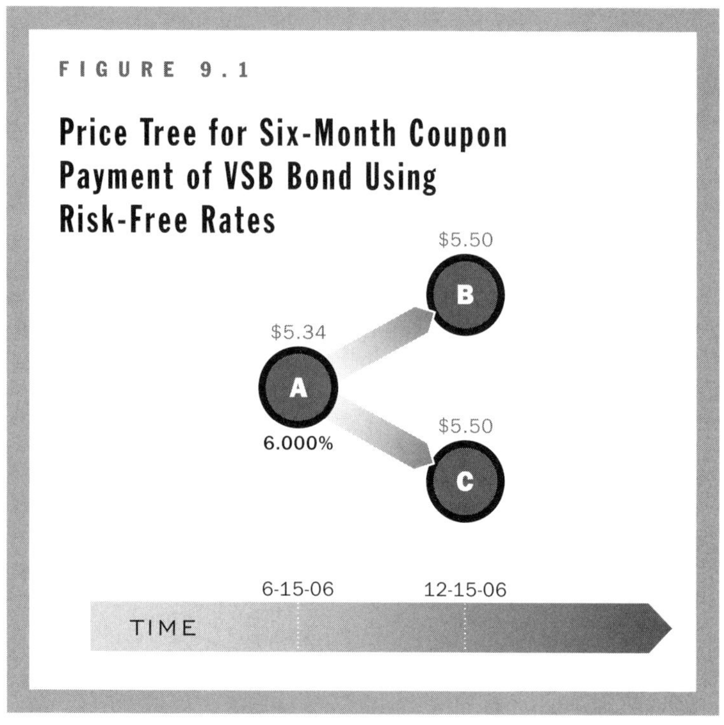

The following evaluation of a bullet bond issued by the fictitious Victoria School Bus Corporation (VSB Corp.) illustrates the spread-measurement process. The assumption is that this bond pays a semiannual 11 percent coupon, matures on 12/15/07, and carries a single-A credit rating. The objective is to measure the incremental return associated with a $100 face amount at an observed market price of $103.50 for settlement on 6/15/06.

As in Chapter 8, a model-predicted price is generated by separately present-valuing each of the bond's future cash flows through the binomial tree and then combining their values to arrive at a price for the bond as a whole on the 6/15/06 settlement date. The VSB bond's cash flows include $5.50 coupon payments to be made on 12/15/06 and 6/15/07, and a $105.50 coupon and principal payment to be made at maturity on 12/15/07. Initially, each of these cash flows is present-valued using the risk-free rates in the calibrated binomial tree from Chapter 8. **FIGURE 9.1** shows the price tree for the \$5.50 six-month coupon payment to be made on 12/15/06. Using equation 8.2, the model calculates the 6/15/06 price for the six-month cash flow as follows:

$$P_{1,A \text{ six-month cash flow}} = \frac{(\$5.50 + \$5.50)}{2} \times \frac{1}{(1 + \frac{0.06000}{2})}$$

$$= \$5.34$$

FIGURE 9.2 repeats this process for the \$5.50 one-year coupon payment. On its 6/15/07 payment date, the cash flow's price is

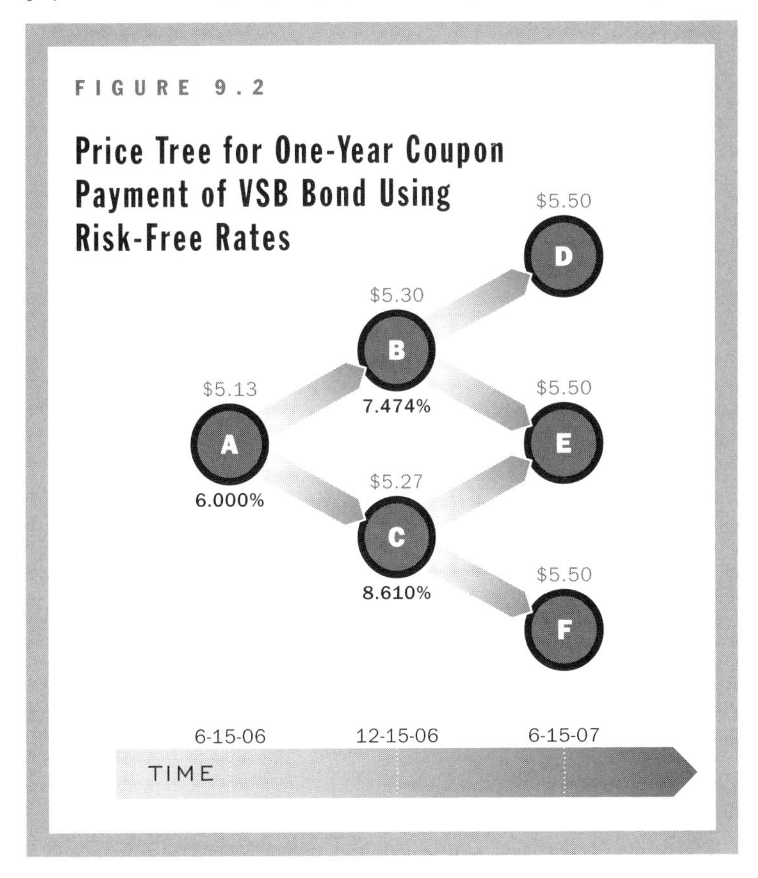

\$5.50 at all nodes (*D*, *E*, and *F*). Six months before payment, on 12/15/06, equation 8.2 gives prices of \$5.30 at node *B* and \$5.27 at node *C*. Applying equation 8.2 once more gives the one-year cash flow's value on 6/15/06:

$$P_{1,A \text{ one-year cash flow}} = \frac{(\$5.30 + \$5.27)}{2} \times \frac{1}{(1 + \frac{0.06000}{2})}$$
$$= \$5.13$$

The VSB bond's 1.5-year coupon and principal payment has a value of \$105.50 on 12/15/07, shown at nodes *G*, *H*, *I*, and *J* in **FIGURE 9.3**. These values, in conjunction with the short rates at nodes *D*, *E*, and *F*, give prices of \$101.07 (at *D*), \$100.43 (at *E*), and \$99.70 (at *F*) on 6/15/07. Similarly, prices of \$97.12 and \$95.93 are determined for nodes *B* and *C*, respectively, on 12/15/06. The determination of the 6/15/06 value of this cash flow is shown below:

$$P_{1,A \text{ 1.5-year cash flow}} = \frac{(\$97.12 + \$95.93)}{2} \times \frac{1}{(1 + \frac{0.06000}{2})}$$
$$= \$93.72$$

The model-predicted price for the VSB bond is calculated by adding together the 6/15/06 values of its cash flows:

$$P_{\text{model-predicted}} = \$5.34 + \$5.13 + \$93.72 = \$104.19$$

Thus, with no spread estimate, the calibrated model generates a price of \$104.19 for the bond. *If this were the observed price of the issue, we would conclude that the issue provides no incremental return relative to risk-free short rates.*

But the observed price is \$103.50, not \$104.19. To determine the incremental return, or spread, associated with \$103.50, the rates in the model must be altered until they generate this price. The alteration takes the form of a constant spread applied to each of the short rates in the binomial tree. Applying a positive con-

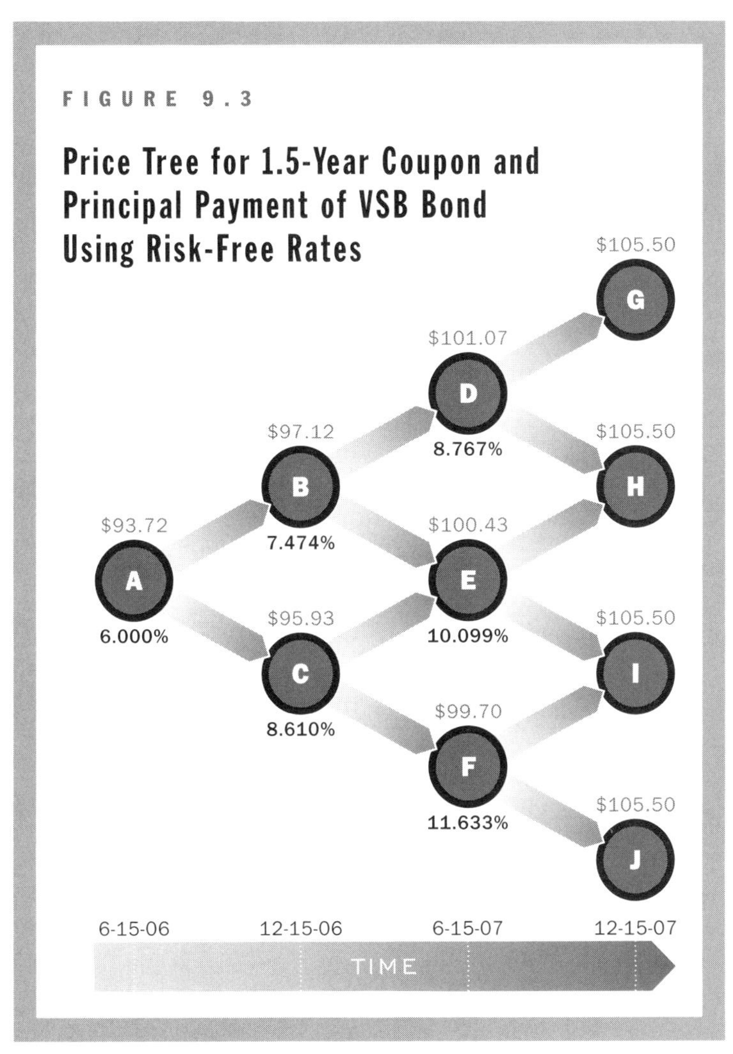

FIGURE 9.3

Price Tree for 1.5-Year Coupon and Principal Payment of VSB Bond Using Risk-Free Rates

stant spread will increase the short rates in the model, increase the discounting of the cash flows, and generate a *lower* security price; a negative spread will decrease rates and generate a higher price.

Each time a spread estimate is made, the individual cash flows of the bond must be repriced using the rates in the tree plus

EQUATION 9.1

Binomial-Tree Price Equation Incorporating Spread

$$P_{j,i} = \frac{(P_{j+1,i+1} + P_{j+1,i})}{2} \times \frac{1}{\left(1 + \frac{(f_{j,i} + s)}{2}\right)}$$

Where:

$P_{j,i}$ = Price of cash flow on date j, at node i

$P_{j+1,i+1}$ = Price of cash flow one period in the future from date j, on date $j+1$, at node $i+1$

$P_{j+1,i}$ = Price of cash flow on date $j+1$, at node i

$f_{j,i}$ = Short rate for period commencing on date j, at node i (decimal)

s = Spread added to each short rate in the binomial tree (decimal)

this spread. Since the spread is added to each rate in the tree, it may be incorporated into equation 8.2, the general formula for determining a cash flow's price at a given node in the binomial tree. The modified formula is shown as **EQUATION 9.1**.

In equation 9.1, the spread factor, s, is added to the short rate $f_{j,i}$ in the denominator of the formula. As previously stated, a positive spread will increase the rate at which a given cash flow is discounted, causing its present value to decrease, whereas a negative spread will cause the present value to increase. Since the VSB bond's $104.19 model-predicted price is greater than its $103.50 observed price, the rates in the tree must be increased by applying a positive spread.

After successive trial-and-error estimates, it was found that a uniform spread of +48.5 basis points caused the model to generate the desired \$103.50 price for the VSB bond. **FIGURE 9.4** shows the price tree for the six-month coupon payment using risk-free rates plus the positive 48.5bp spread. Here is the price calculation that incorporates this spread:

$$P_{1,A\text{ six-month cash flow}} = \frac{(P_{2,B} + P_{2,C})}{2} \times \frac{1}{(1 + \frac{f_{1,A} + s}{2})}$$

$$= \frac{(\$5.50 + \$5.50)}{2} \times \frac{1}{(1 + \frac{0.06000 + 0.00485}{2})}$$

$$= \frac{(\$5.50 + \$5.50)}{2} \times \frac{1}{(1 + \frac{0.06485}{2})}$$

$$= \$5.33$$

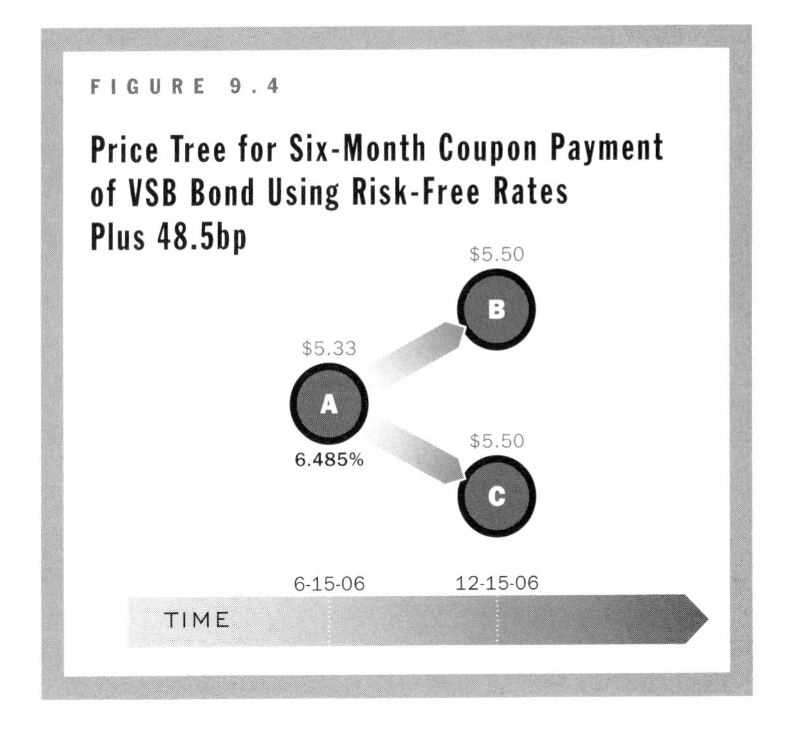

FIGURE 9.4

Price Tree for Six-Month Coupon Payment of VSB Bond Using Risk-Free Rates Plus 48.5bp

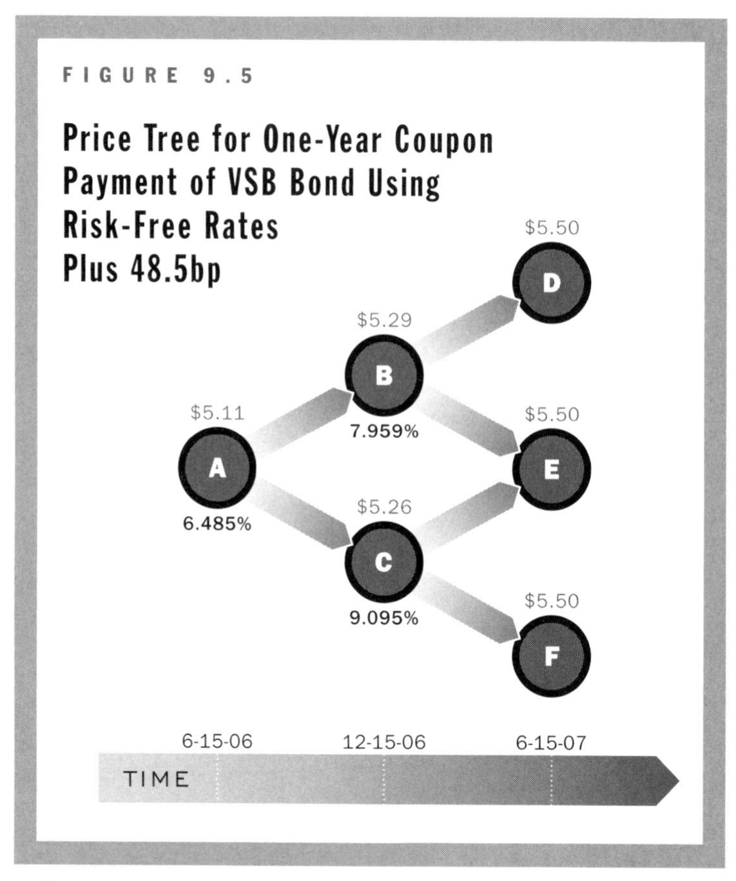

FIGURE 9.5

Price Tree for One-Year Coupon Payment of VSB Bond Using Risk-Free Rates Plus 48.5bp

Increasing the short rate at node *A* by 48.5bp caused the present value of the six-month coupon payment to drop from $5.34 to $5.33. **FIGURE 9.5** shows a similar price tree for the one-year coupon payment. In this case, the rates at nodes *B* and *C*, 7.474 and 8.610 percent, have been increased by 48.5bp, to 7.959 and 9.095 percent. The prices at nodes *B* and *C* are determined accordingly:

$$P_{2,B\text{ one-year cash flow}} = \frac{(\$5.50 + \$5.50)}{2} \times \frac{1}{(1 + \frac{0.07474 + 0.00485}{2})}$$

$$= \$5.29$$

$$P_{2,C\text{ one-year cash flow}} = \frac{(\$5.50 + \$5.50)}{2} \times \frac{1}{(1 + \frac{0.0861 + 0.00485}{2})}$$

$$= \$5.26$$

Using the above prices, the 6/15/06 value of this cash flow is determined below:

$$P_{1,A\text{ one-year cash flow}} = \frac{(\$5.29 + \$5.26)}{2} \times \frac{1}{(1 + \frac{0.06000 + 0.00485}{2})}$$

$$= \$5.11$$

Lastly, the 1.5-year cash flow's price tree, **FIGURE 9.6**, shows that this cash flow has a value of $93.06 on 6/15/06. The model-predicted price for the VSB bond using risk-free rates plus a positive spread of 48.5bp is determined below:

$$P_{\text{model-predicted}} = \$5.33 + \$5.11 + \$93.06 = \$103.50$$

Since the model-predicted price matches the issue's observed price, we may conclude that the VSB bond, at $103.50, provides an incremental return of +48.5 basis points over the risk-free short rates in the model. Since these rates describe risk-free returns over successive time periods, taken together they describe the risk-free rate of return over the term under consideration, 1.5 years in this case. *The +48.5bp spread, therefore, represents the additional return expected to be generated by the VSB bond over this term relative to risk-free returns.*

A spread derived in this manner is often referred to as the **option-adjusted spread (OAS)** of a bullet bond. We refrain from using this term here, to emphasize that such an issue does not contain an embedded option and therefore does not have a spread that has been "adjusted" to account for one.

Because implied spot rates are derived from benchmark bonds' observed prices and yields, these rates will correctly price the cash

FIGURE 9.6

Price Tree for 1.5-Year Coupon and Principal Payment of VSB Bond Using Risk-Free Short Rates Plus 48.5bp

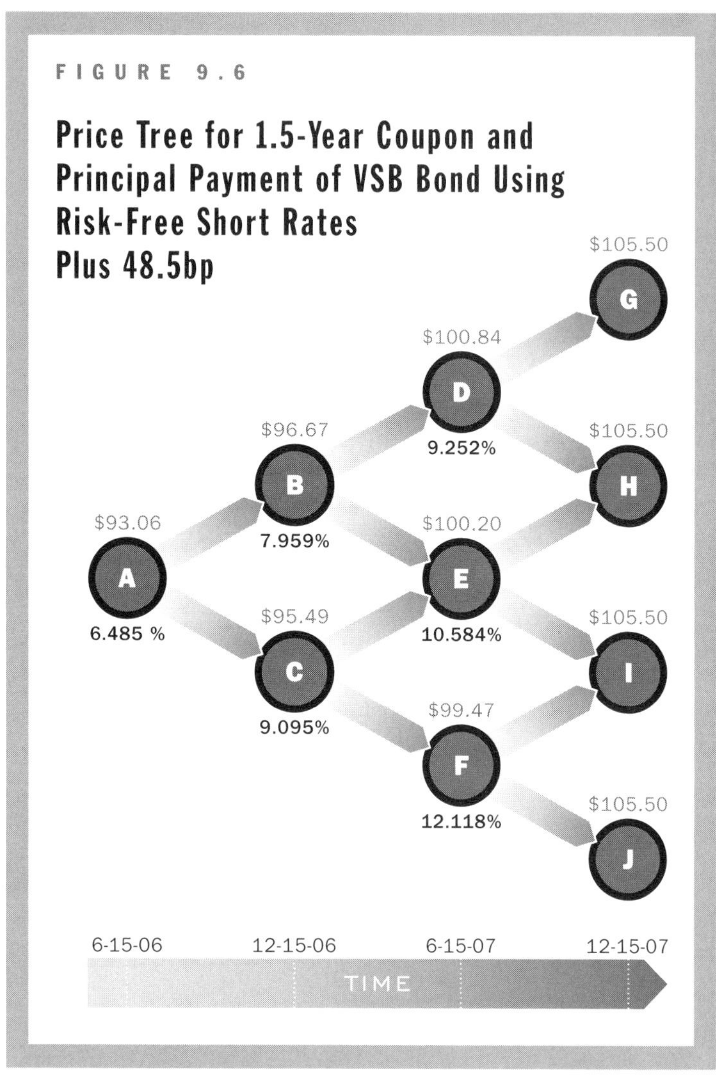

flows of a given benchmark bond, generating a model price that matches the observed value. Since the ability of the binomial tree's short rates to price benchmark bonds correctly was the criterion used to calibrate the tree, the model-determined spread of a non-benchmark issue, when added to the appropriate spot rates, will

EQUATION 9.2

$$PV = FV/\left[\left(1 + \frac{(s_j + s)}{m}\right)^{(n \times m)}\right]$$

Where:

PV = Present value

FV = Future value

s_j = Implied benchmark spot rate (decimal) for period $_j$

s = Spread added to each short rate in the binomial tree (decimal)

m = Number of compounding periods per year

n = Length of period in years

generate the observed price of the nonbenchmark bond. For this reason, the spread determined by the binomial model is often viewed as a uniform spread applied to implied benchmark spot rates and is again interpreted as the incremental return of a bond.

This interpretation of a bond's spread can be demonstrated with the current example of the VSB issue. In this exercise, the spread, s, is added to the implied benchmark spot rate, s_j, of equation 5.1. The resulting expression is shown as **EQUATION 9.2**.

The present values of the VSB bond's 6-month, 1-year, and 1.5-year coupon payments, according to equation 9.2, are shown below. In this example, the 6-month coupon payment is present-valued at the implied 6-month spot rate plus 48.5bp, the 1-year coupon payment at the implied 1-year spot rate plus 48.5bp, and the 1.5-year coupon and principal payment at the 1.5-year implied spot rate plus 48.5bp:

$$PV_{\text{six-month cash flow}} = \$5.50/[1 + (0.06000 + 0.00485)/2]^{(0.5 \times 2)}$$
$$= \$5.33$$

$$PV_{\text{one-year cash flow}} = \$5.50/[1 + (0.07018 + 0.00485)/2]^{(1.0 \times 2)}$$
$$= \$5.11$$

$$PV_{1.5\text{-year cash flow}} = \$105.50/[1 + (0.08054 + 0.00485)/2]^{(1.5\times 2)}$$
$$= \$93.06$$

Combining the present values of the three cash flows gives a total price for the bond of $103.50, as shown below:

$$PV_{bond} = \$5.33 + \$5.11 + \$93.06 = \$103.50$$

Since this price matches the observed price of the bond, the interpretation of the 48.5bp spread as a spread to implied benchmark spot rates is a valid one.

As a point of comparison, consider the conventional yield spread associated with the VSB bond. At a price of $103.50 for settlement on 6/15/06, this 1.5-year issue has an 8.466 percent yield to maturity. Since the 1.5-year benchmark bond has a yield of 8.000 percent, the VSB bond has a *yield spread* of 46.6 basis points at a price of $103.50. In this analysis, an underlying risk-free rate of 8.000 percent plus a yield spread of 46.6bp is used to present-value each cash flow, in effect assuming a flat benchmark yield curve fixed at 8.000 percent. In contrast, the binomial tree incorporates the actual slope of the yield curve (the *true* term structure) in its analysis by utilizing the spot and forward rates implied by this curve.

In addition, note the similarity between the bond's 48.5bp spread to the model's short rates and its 46.6bp yield spread. The 48.5bp spread can be thought of as a spread to a positively sloped **implied spot curve**. In this interpretation, each cash flow is discounted at a unique rate equal to the implied spot rate for its term plus the 48.5bp spread: 6.485 percent for the 6-month cash flow, 7.503 percent for the 1-year cash flow, and 8.539 percent for the 1.5-year cash flow.

In contrast, the yield analysis uses a constant rate of (8.000 + 0.466 =) 8.466 percent for all cash flows. The 8.000 percent benchmark rate with which the VSB bond's yield is compared is selected on the basis of the term of the VSB bond's final principal and interest payment. Since this cash flow represents the largest portion of the bond's present value, and since the underlying benchmark rates associated with this cash flow in the two analyses—8.054 implied benchmark spot rate and the 8.000 benchmark yield—are similar, the spreads associated with the bond in the two analyses are similar.

Regardless of the way in which the spread of a bond is determined, potential investors must decide whether its incremental return provides adequate compensation for the risks it contains. The single-A credit rating of the VSB bond indicates that it contains a degree of default risk. A potential investor would have to decide whether its 48.5bp spread to the binomial tree's short rates or its 46.6bp yield spread is appropriate for its level of risk. One approach to making this decision would be to compare the incremental return of this particular bond with the spreads associated with a broad sampling of similar bonds. Any spread is a *relative* measure.

Measuring the VSB bond's spread to the short rates in the binomial tree entailed present-valuing each cash flow over successive future time periods, beginning on the payment date of a cash flow, when its value is known with certainty, and working back toward the present-valuation date. Since a cash flow's price at a given node in the tree depends on its prices one period in the future, the model generates a distribution of prices for the cash flow on periodic future dates. Therefore, combining all the cash flows' values at a particular node will give a price for the bond as a whole at that node.

Repeating this procedure at all nodes in the tree creates a distribution of future prices for the bond. These future prices depend on the underlying benchmark yield curve, which determines the implied forward rates; the assumed volatility rate, which helps determine each period's short rates; and the current price of the bond, which governs the issue's spread. The cash-flow price trees that incorporate all these factors are used to generate the bond's price tree.

FIGURE 9.7 shows the price tree for the VSB bullet bond as a whole. At each node, the prices from figures 9.4, 9.5, and 9.6 are combined. For example, at node *B*, the prices of the 6-month, 1-year, and 1.5-year cash flows, from figures 9.4, 9.5, and 9.6, are $5.50, $5.29, and $96.67, respectively. Combining these values gives

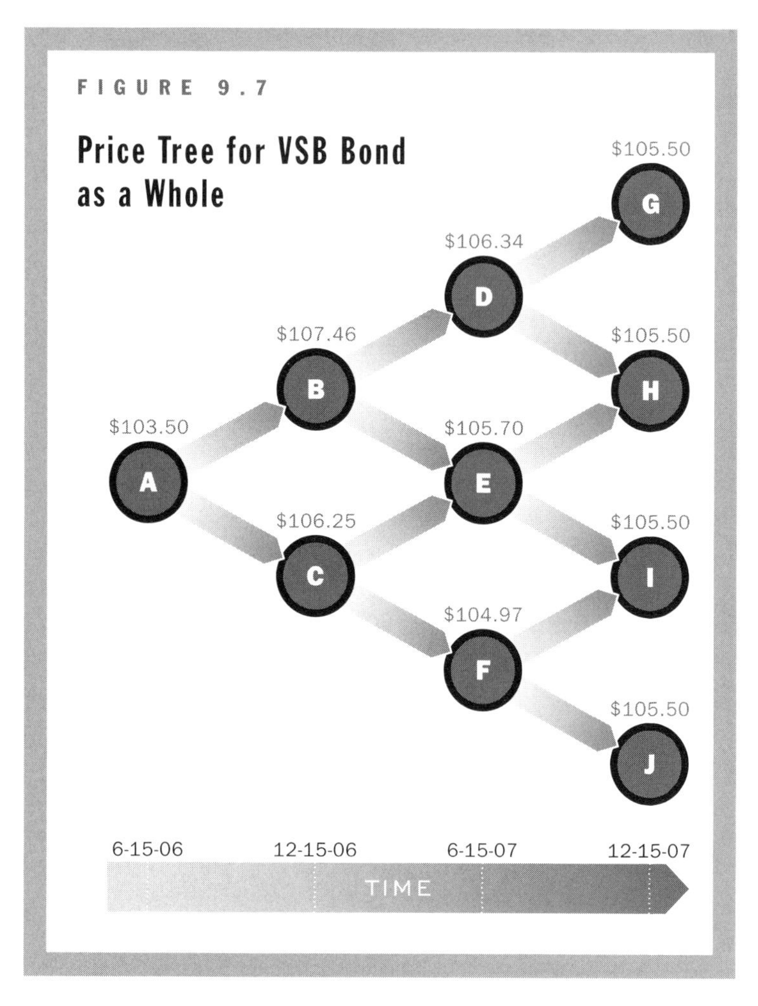

a bond price of $107.46 at node *B*, as shown below:

$$P_{2,B}\text{bond} = P_{2,B\,\text{six-month cash flow}} + P_{2,B\,\text{one-year cash flow}} + P_{2,B\,\text{1.5-year cash flow}}$$

$$= \$5.50 + \$5.29 + \$96.67 = \$107.46$$

Prices at other nodes are found similarly.

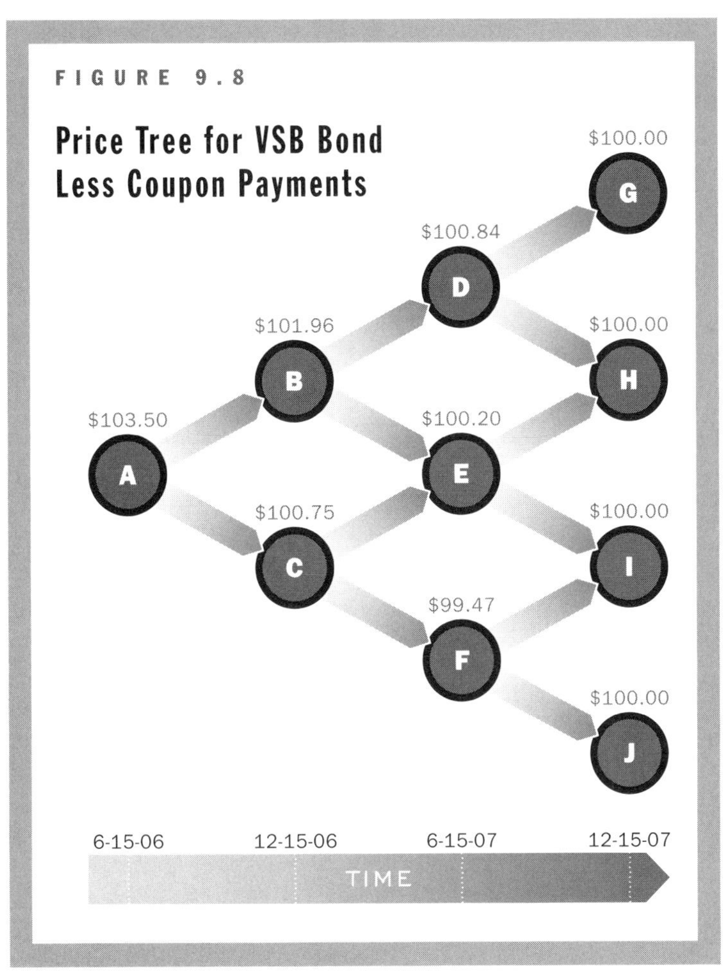

FIGURE 9.8

Price Tree for VSB Bond Less Coupon Payments

Bond prices are quoted less their accrued interest. This is the case at node *A*. At each of the other nodes in the price tree, however, the bond's price includes the coupon payment to be made on that date. For example, at node *B*, the $107.46 bond price includes the $5.50 coupon payment to be made on that date. The value of any coupon payments needs to be removed from these prices. Therefore, bond prices at nodes *B* through *J*, each of which includes a $5.50 coupon payment, are reduced by this amount in order to generate a true price distribution for the VSB bond. For example, removing the $5.50 coupon payment from the bond's $107.46 full price at node *B* results in a price of $101.96. The resulting price tree is shown in **FIGURE 9.8**.

This price tree will play an important role in evaluating the impact of an embedded option on a bond's behavior and return, as the next chapter will show.

CHAPTER 10

NONBULLET BONDS

THE VSB BULLET BOND introduced in Chapter 9 is an example of a fixed-income security whose cash flows are independent of the level of interest rates. In other words, no matter how interest rates change or what values they assume, the VSB bullet bond's future payment stream remains intact and unaffected. In contrast, a large class of fixed-coupon *nonbullet* bonds have payment streams that are dependent on the level of interest rates. For this group of securities, the actual payments made are determined in some way by the interest rates prevailing at a particular point in time. Nonbullet bonds of this type contain one or more provisions for the early return of principal. As discussed earlier, these provisions are referred to as "embedded options."

To illustrate the behavior of a bond with interest-rate-dependent cash flows, this chapter will introduce a call provision into the cash-flow structure of the VSB bond, keeping its price, coupon, and maturity the same. The call is modeled as a discrete par ($100) call that may be exercised only on 6/15/07. As in Chapter 9, the objective is to measure the incremental return associated with the $103.50 observed price of this bond.

If a bond has a call feature, the final principal payment—scheduled to take place on its stated maturity date—may instead take place before this date. When the call provision is exercised, it eliminates all coupon payments scheduled to take place after the call date. In the VSB bond example, the issuer's exercise of the 6/15/07 par call would cause investors to lose the final $5.50 coupon payment scheduled to take place on 12/15/07 and to receive the principal face amount six months earlier than scheduled.

From the investors' standpoint, the presence of a call on a portion of a bond's payment stream is detrimental to the bond's performance. For a sufficient decrease in interest rates, the issuer would call the bond, terminating the investors' source of above-market returns and forcing them to reinvest at the lower prevailing rates. If rates were to rise, the bond would not be called and the investor would be faced with a choice between accepting below-market returns and selling the bond at a reduced price.

In general, a rational issuer will exercise its right to call a bond if the cost of calling is less than the cost of not calling. In the VSB bond example, the cost associated with not calling the bond (ignoring administrative and transaction costs) is the $5.50 final coupon payment on 12/15/07. If VSB Corp. were able to issue another bond that paid a coupon lower than $5.50 on this date, it would call the 11 percent issue on 6/15/07 and replace it with a new issue bearing the lower coupon. This course of action would be available to VSB Corp. if the prevailing interest rate for the outstanding bond on the call's exercise date were *lower* than its coupon.

AS DISCUSSED IN Chapter 2, investors who own the callable VSB bond are long the underlying bullet and short the 6/15/07 par call to VSB Corp. Since the binomial tree models interest rates for future periods, it may be used to identify those interest-rate conditions under which the bond will be called and those under which it will not. The first step in this process is to create a price tree for the callable VSB bond's underlying bullet. This task has already been carried out, and the result is shown in figure 9.8, replicated here as **FIGURE 10.1**.

From the model's perspective, the call option will be exercised when it is in the money, that is, when the underlying bullet bond's

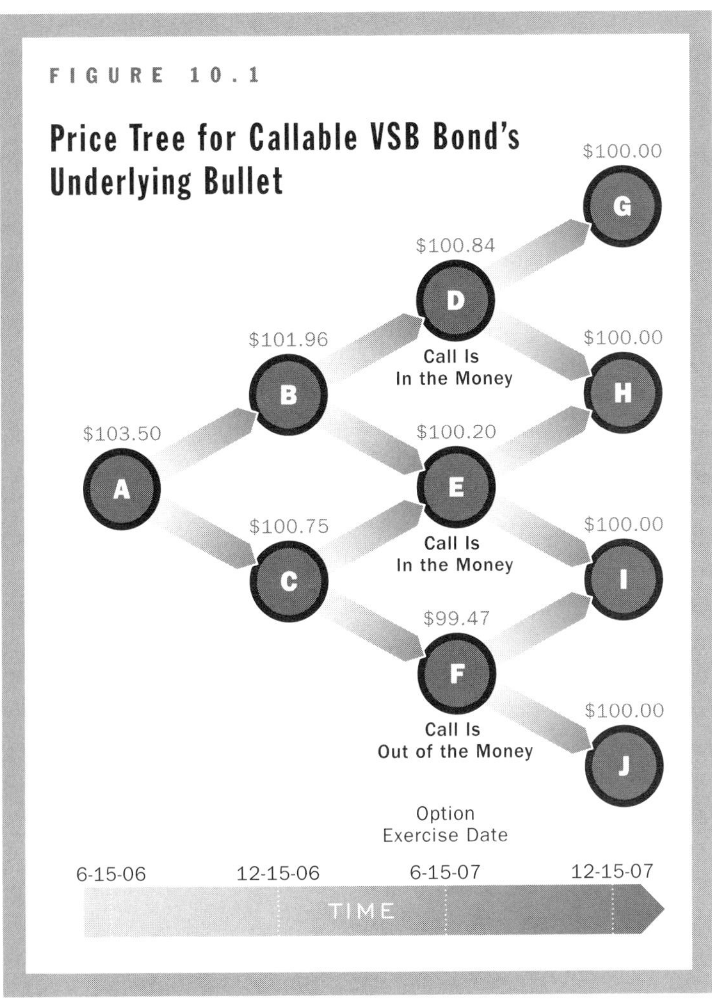

price is greater than the option's \$100 strike price. On 6/15/07, the option's exercise date, the model generates underlying bullet-bond prices of \$100.84 at node *D*, \$100.20 at node *E*, and \$99.47 at node *F*. At nodes *D* and *E*, the par call is in the money and would therefore be exercised by a rational option holder such as VSB Corp. Exercise of the call means that those short the call—the investors—*must* sell the underlying bullet bond to the issuer,

VSB Corp., at the call price, in this case, par. Under these circumstances, the issuer terminates its obligation to pay above-market rates for borrowed capital, while investors are left with a cash payout that must be invested at lower prevailing rates.

The effect of the call may be combined with the underlying bullet bond's price tree to generate a price tree for the actual callable bond. This is done by reconstructing the price tree for each of the bond's cash flows, incorporating the effect of the call where appropriate. Since the six-month and one-year coupon payments occur prior to or on the option's exercise date, they will be paid whether or not the option is exercised. As a result, their price trees are unaffected by the option on the bond and remain unchanged from figures 9.4 and 9.5.

Since the 1.5-year cash flow's payment is scheduled to occur after the option's exercise date, its behavior depends on whether or not the bond is called. Because this is the only remaining cash flow on 6/15/07, its price represents the price of the bond as a whole (less coupon payments) on that date. As previously stated, the underlying bullet will be called at nodes containing prices greater than the embedded option's $100 strike price on 6/15/07. Therefore, the maximum price of the callable bond on 6/15/07 is $100. As a result, any node that contains a price greater than $100 for the underlying bullet is replaced with the lower $100 call price for the actual callable bond. The price tree for the 1.5-year payment, modified from figure 9.6 to reflect this maximum price, is shown in **FIGURE 10.2.**

At nodes *D* and *E*, the $100.84 and $100.20 premium prices have been crossed out and replaced with the maximum $100 call price. Paths *DG*, *DH*, *EH*, and *EI* are eliminated, since a bond called at node *D* or *E* would not exist after 6/15/07 and therefore could not arrive at nodes *G*, *H*, or *I* by these paths. The lowered prices at *D* and *E* cause the prices at nodes *B* and *C* to decline when recalculated according to equation 9.1. Thus, the $97.67 price at node *B* is reduced to $96.17, and the $95.49 price at node *C* is reduced to $95.40. Lastly, the lower values at *B* and *C* cause the 6/15/06 value of this cash flow at node *A* to decrease from $93.06 to $92.78.

With a new price tree for the cash flow affected by the call con-

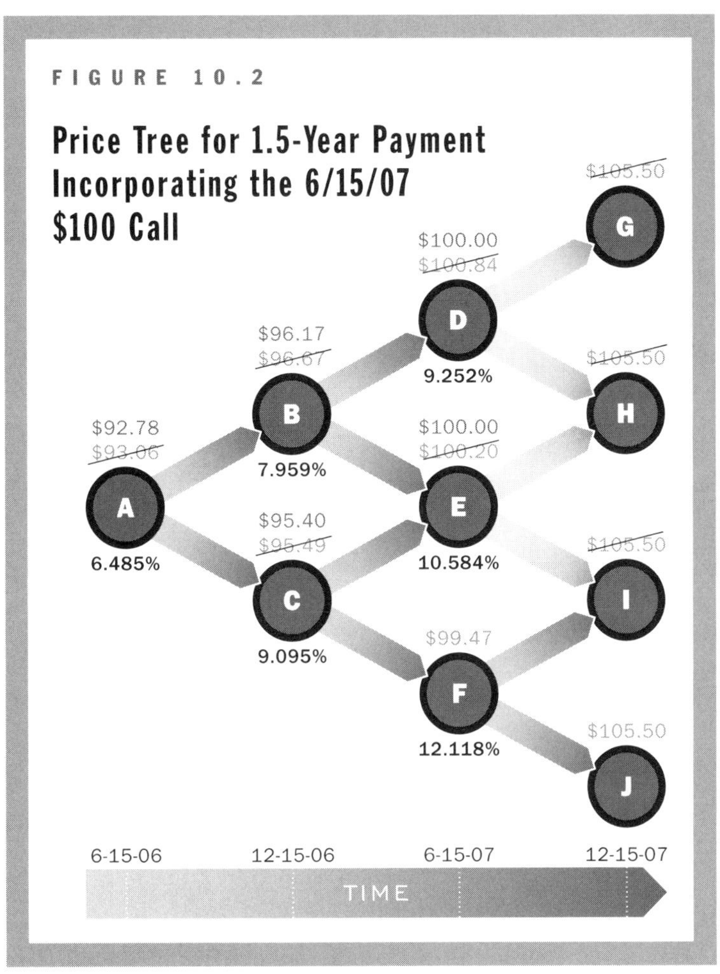

FIGURE 10.2

Price Tree for 1.5-Year Payment Incorporating the 6/15/07 $100 Call

structed, a price tree for the callable bond as a whole may be generated. As in Chapter 9, all the cash flows' values at a particular node are combined to give a price for the bond as a whole at that node. For example, from figures 9.4 and 9.5, the 6-month and 1-year payments have values of $5.50 and $5.29, respectively, at node *B*. From figure 10.2, the 1.5-year payment's value at this node is $96.17. Combining these values gives the callable bond's full price at node *B*, as shown below:

$$P_{2,B\,\text{callable bond (full)}} = \$5.50 + \$5.29 + \$96.17$$
$$= \$106.96$$

The price of the bond less accrued interest is found by subtracting the \$5.50 coupon payment to be made on 12/15/06 from the full price of the bond:

$$P_{2,B\,\text{callable bond}} = \$106.96 - \$5.50 = \$101.46$$

FIGURE 10.3

Price Tree for Callable VSB Bond Less Coupon Payments

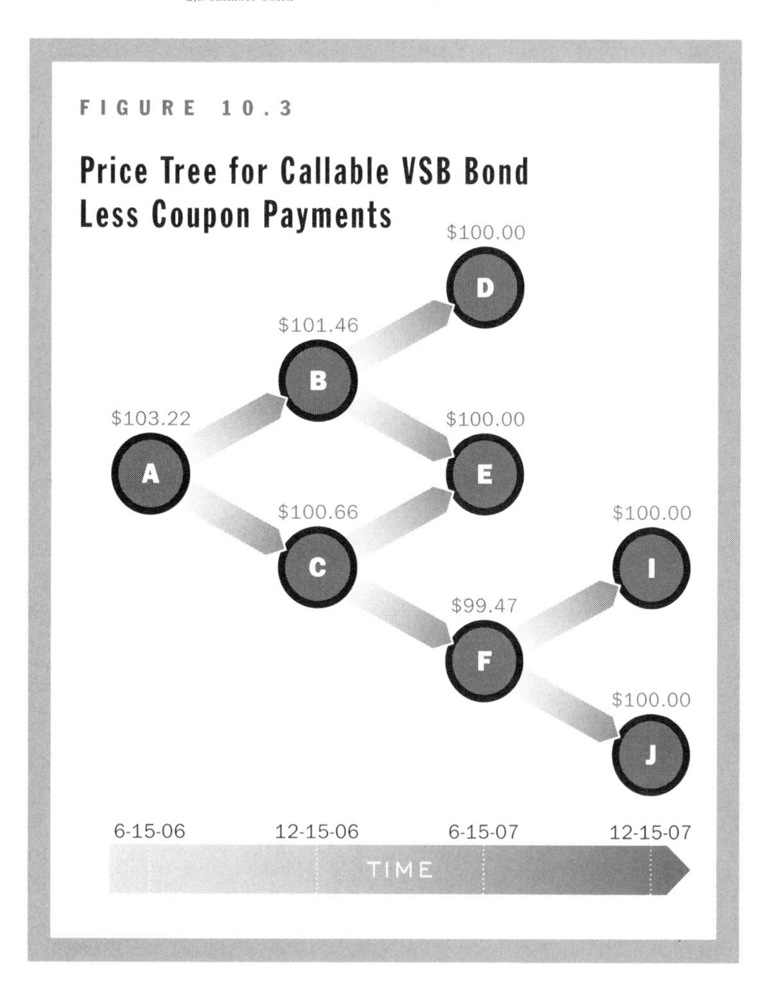

Prices at all the other nodes are determined similarly and are shown in **FIGURE 10.3**, the price tree for the callable VSB bond less coupon payments. At node *A*, the model-generated price for the bond is shown to be $103.22.

The price trees developed in Chapter 9 are used in constructing the price tree for the callable bond. As found in these earlier trees, the bullet VSB bond provided a spread of 48.5 basis points at a price of $103.50. This spread was then incorporated into the price trees for the *callable* bond's cash flows as well, producing the price of $103.22.

Why does a 48.5bp spread imply a $103.22 price for the callable bond and a higher $103.50 price for the bullet bond? When analyzing the bullet issue, the model-generated price was decreased by adding a spread to the risk-free short rates in the tree until a price

FIGURE 10.4

Price Tree for Six-Month Coupon Payment of Callable VSB Bond Using Risk-Free Rates Plus 23.5bp

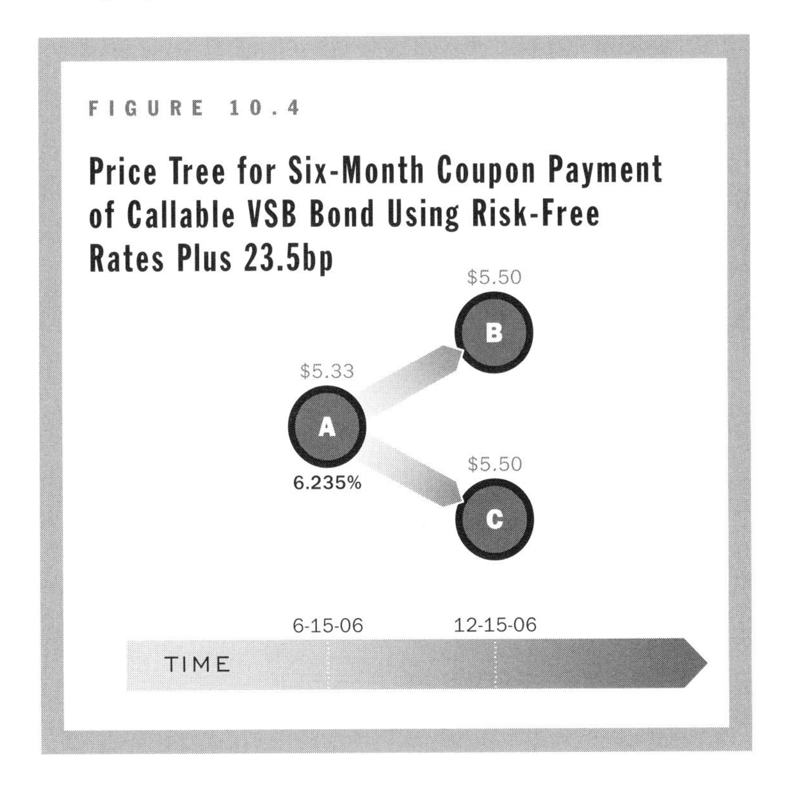

was generated that matched the one to be evaluated. In pricing the callable bond, the same 48.5bp spread to the short rates was added. In addition, however, the prices in the tree for the 1.5-year cash flow were manually lowered because of the maximum price—$100—imposed by the call. The combination of the 48.5bp spread and the call-reduced prices caused the model to generate a price for the callable bond that is *lower* than its observed price.

Intuitively, the lower price for the callable bond results from the loss of a portion of the bond's future value because of the call

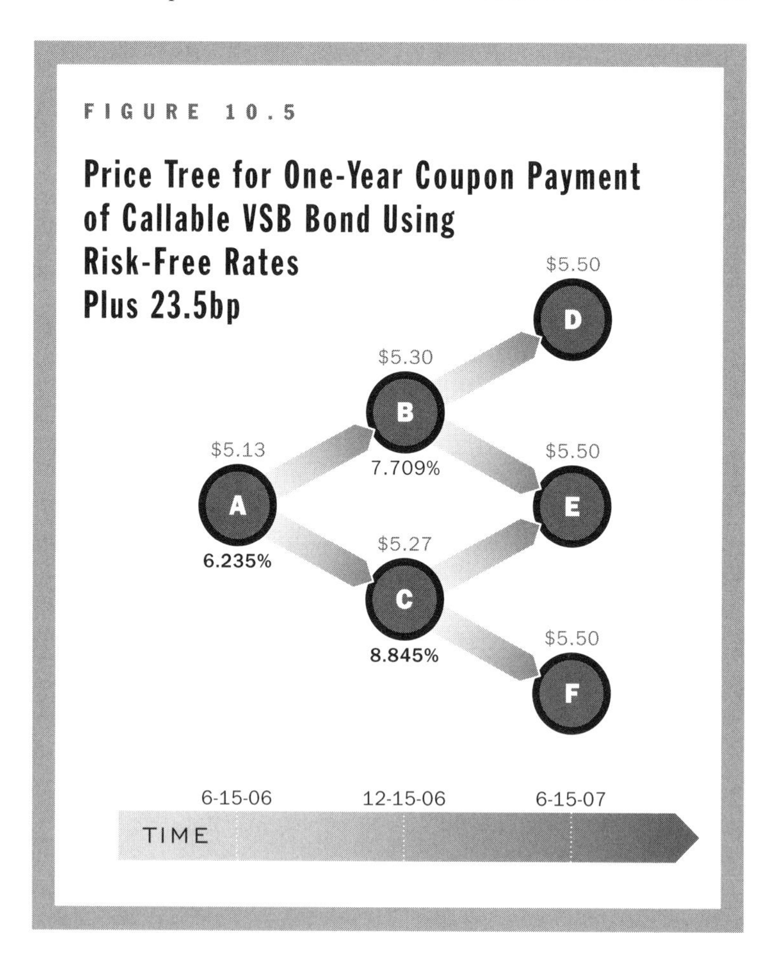

FIGURE 10.5

Price Tree for One-Year Coupon Payment of Callable VSB Bond Using Risk-Free Rates Plus 23.5bp

at nodes *D* and *E*. For the bond to provide the same incremental return as the bullet, it would have to be purchased at a lower price.

To determine the incremental spread associated with the callable bond's \$103.50 observed price, the spread estimate must be adjusted so that the model generates this price. Since the model price of the issue must be raised from \$103.22 to \$103.50, the spread must be reduced on a trial-and-error basis until the appropriate value is found. As in previous examples, each cash flow must be repriced using each spread estimate.

After a number of trials, it was found that reducing the spread from 48.5bp to 23.5bp caused the model to generate the desired price of \$103.50. **FIGURES 10.4** and **10.5** show the price trees of the 6-month and 1-year cash flows of the callable VSB bond using risk-free short rates plus the 23.5bp spread. **FIGURE 10.6** shows a similar tree for the 1.5-year cash flow, with the appropriate price reductions caused by the call. The model-generated price for the bond is found by once again combining all the trees' 6/15/06 prices at node *A*:

$$P_{\text{model-predicted}} = \$5.33 + \$5.13 + \$93.04 = \$103.50$$

FIGURE 10.7 shows the price tree for the bond as a whole (less coupon payments). The model-generated price of \$103.50 is shown at node *A*.

Given the callable VSB bond's cash-flow structure and \$103.50 price, 10 percent volatility, and the benchmark yield curve shown in table 5.2, this bond has an option-adjusted spread (OAS) of 23.5 basis points to the binomial tree's risk-free short rates. This spread is lower than that of the bullet because the expected return of the callable issue has been adjusted for the disadvantageous impact of the embedded call option. In other words, at the same price as the bullet bond, the callable bond would be expected to underperform the bullet; at the same OAS, it has a lower 6/15/06 price.

The callable bond's inability to provide an expected return equal to that of its bullet counterpart is a result of the cap imposed

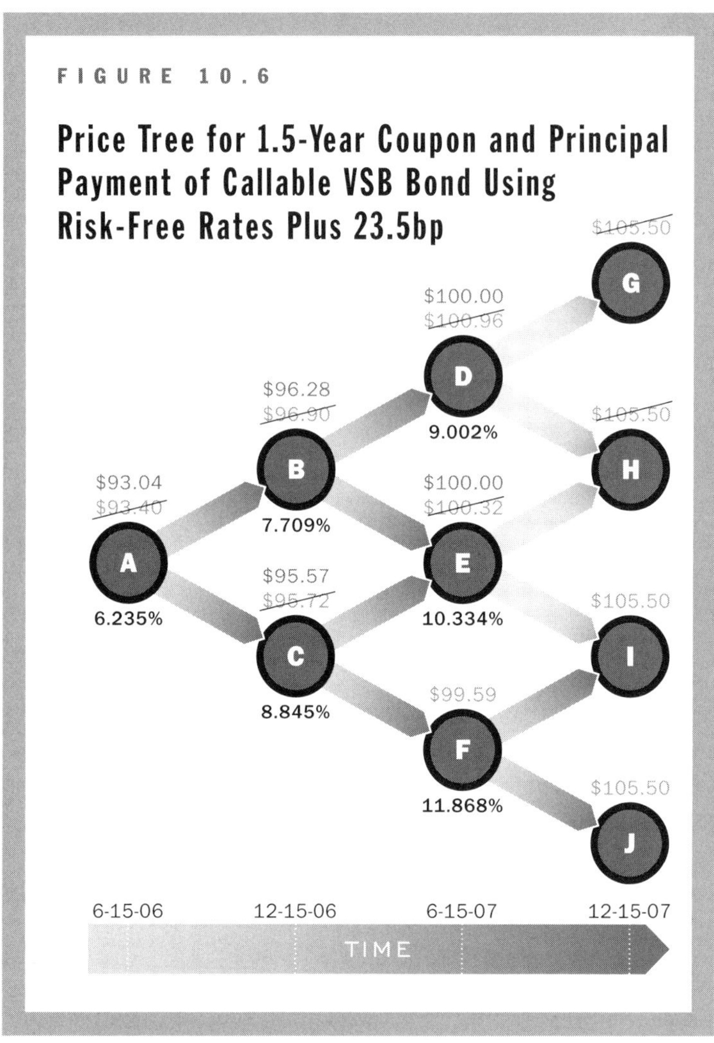

FIGURE 10.6

Price Tree for 1.5-Year Coupon and Principal Payment of Callable VSB Bond Using Risk-Free Rates Plus 23.5bp

on its price by the embedded call. If, instead, the bond contained a put, the opposite effect would take place. Once again, a rational option holder—the investor, in this case—would exercise the put when it was in the money, that is, when the underlying bullet's price was below the embedded put's strike price. Here, the put would act as a floor to the put bond's price. The option-adjusted

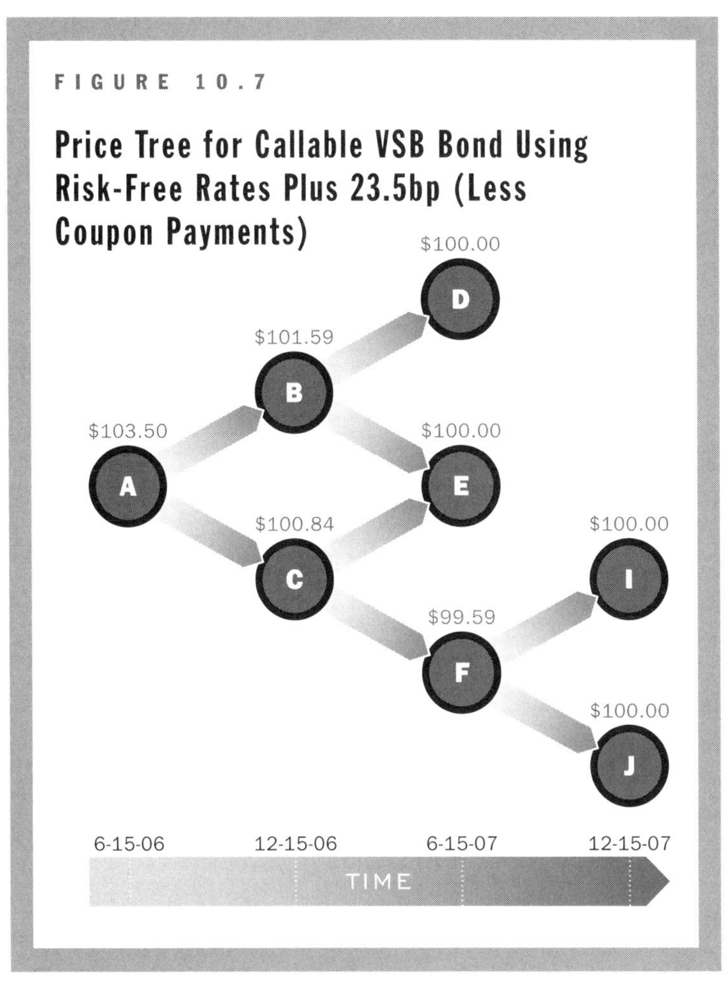

FIGURE 10.7

Price Tree for Callable VSB Bond Using Risk-Free Rates Plus 23.5bp (Less Coupon Payments)

spread of this security would be greater than the spread of the underlying bullet, because the embedded put would limit the put bond's price decline under otherwise adverse circumstances.

WITH THE NONBULLET bond's OAS determined, it is useful to derive a monetary value for the issue's embedded option. This value is determined by measuring the intrinsic value of the option on its future exercise date relative to the underlying bullet bond's

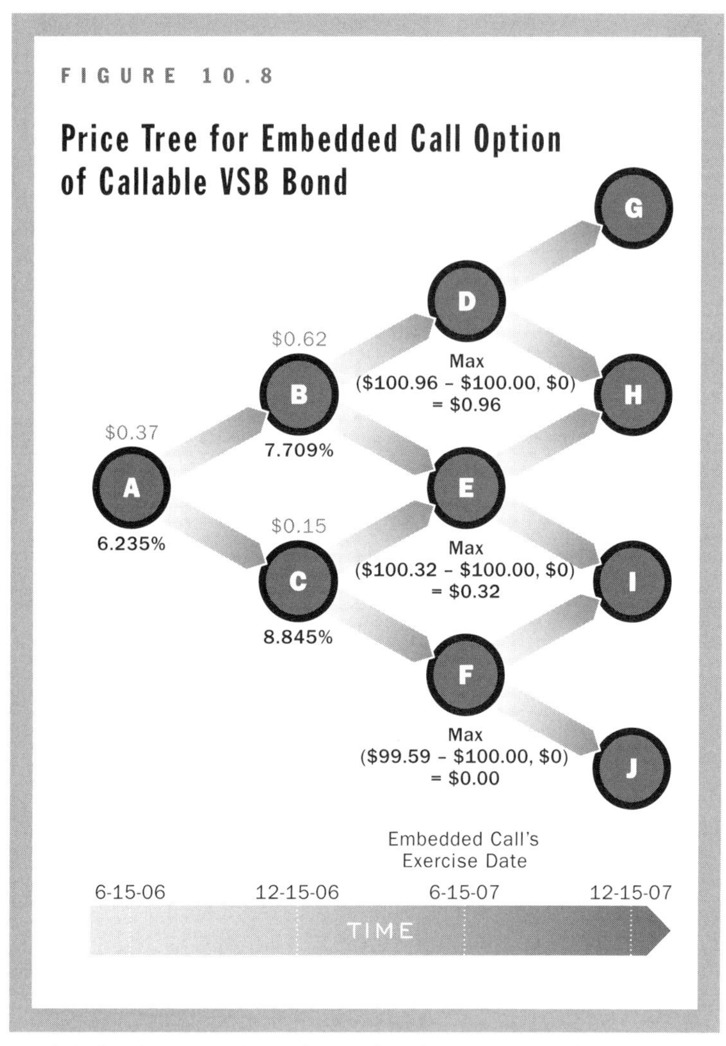

modeled price at each node on this date. Any resulting intrinsic value is then present-valued through the binomial tree to arrive at the option's current value. As previously stated, the present value of an option's expected future value is referred to as its time value. **FIGURE 10.8** shows the price tree for the callable VSB bond's embedded option, determined using the principles outlined above.

EQUATION 10.1

Intrinsic Value of Call Option

$$c_i = MAX[(P_{ub} - E), 0]$$

Where: c_i = Intrinsic value of the call option
MAX[ ] = Maximum, or greater, of the values listed between the brackets
P_{ub} = Price of underlying bullet
E = Call option's exercise, or strike, price

Although figure 10.6 represents the price tree for the final cash flow, it also represents the price tree for the bond as a whole on 6/15/07. Thus, this figure shows that the underlying bullet has a model price of $100.96 at node *D*. The intrinsic value of the call is the greater of the underlying bond's price less the call price and zero. This relationship is shown arithmetically as **EQUATION 10.1**.

Equation 10.1 states that an option's value is measured by the extent to which it is in the money. Since option holders are not obligated to exercise, they will do so only when it generates a profit, that is, when the option is in the money. When the option is out of the money, exercise is unprofitable and so will not occur. As a result, the minimum value of an option is zero.

Applying equation 10.1 at node *D* gives the intrinsic value of the embedded call at this node:

$$\begin{aligned} c_i = c_{3,D} &= MAX[(\$100.96 - \$100.00), 0] \\ &= MAX[\$0.96, 0] \\ &= \$0.96 \end{aligned}$$

Similarly, the option has an intrinsic value of $0.32 at node *E*. At node *F*, the option is out of the money because the underlying bond's price is lower than the option's strike price. As a result, the embedded call has an intrinsic value of $0.

With the option's intrinsic value at the various nodes on its exercise date established, the next step is to present-value these quantities through the tree. This is accomplished by the same means used to present-value the bond's cash flows and utilizes the same risk-free rates and 23.5bp spread used to price the callable bond. Adapting equation 9.1 to price the embedded call at node *B* and designating its value as c gives:

$$c_{2,B} = \frac{(c_{3,D} + c_{3,E})}{2} \times \frac{1}{(1 + \frac{f_{2,B} + s}{2})}$$

$$= \frac{(\$0.96 + \$0.32)}{2} \times \frac{1}{(1 + \frac{0.07474 + 0.00235}{2})}$$

$$= \$0.62$$

Similarly, the option's value at node *C* is determined as \$0.15. Repeating this procedure for node *A* gives the embedded call a value of \$0.37 on 6/15/06. Since this option cannot be exercised on 6/15/06, the \$0.37 value is viewed as its time value.

If the bond were also callable on 12/15/06, as in the case of a discretely callable bond with multiple call dates or a continuously callable bond, the option's intrinsic value at node *B* would be determined in the same manner as that used for the 6/15/07 exercise date. This value would then be compared with the \$0.62 value determined from the 6/15/07 call date. The option's value at node *B* is taken as the greater of the two values. If the intrinsic value at node *B* were greater than \$0.62, it would replace the \$0.62 value currently at node *B*; if it were less, the \$0.62 value would be retained at node *B*.

PART FIVE

Applications of OAS Analysis

CHAPTER 11

EVALUATING PERFORMANCE

CHAPTER 10 FOCUSED on how to determine the option-adjusted spread and embedded option value of a nonbullet bond. This chapter will discuss how the scope of the analysis may be extended to draw further insights into a bond's performance. The discussion will be facilitated by considering $100 face amount of the Pacific Bell (AT&T) 6.625% bond due 10/15/34.

This issue, introduced in Chapter 1, contains a provision allowing Pacific Bell (AT&T) to call the bonds on or any time after 10/15/13, twenty years before maturity. **TABLE 11.1** shows an option-adjusted spread (OAS) analysis for this bond. At a price of $100.45 and an assumed volatility of 12.6 percent per year, the Pacific Bell (AT&T) bond has an OAS of +76.2 basis points and an embedded call-option value of $8.49. These values are arrived at using the methodologies discussed in Chapter 10, in conjunction with the benchmark yield curve shown in the table and settlement on 11/20/06.

If an owner of this callable bond were able to buy back this bond's embedded call, he would close out his short position in the call and be left with a bullet bond. The total cost of the bullet would therefore equal the sum of the costs of the callable bond, $100.45, and the option, $8.49. Since the Pacific Bell (AT&T) bond's price

TABLE 11.1

Option-Adjusted Spread Analysis

Pacific Bell (AT&T) CUSIP: 694032AX1
6.625% Callable Bond Due 10/15/34

INPUTS		
Settlement Date:		11/20/06
Price:		100.45% of face amount
Volatility:		12.6%
Term	**Reference Curve**	**Yield (%)**
3 mo		5.365
6 mo		5.380
1 yr		5.302
2 yr		5.067
3 yr		4.980
4 yr		4.971
5 yr		4.979
7 yr		5.012
10 yr		5.069
20 yr		5.199
30 yr		5.213

OUTPUTS OF LOGNORMAL MODEL

Option-Adjusted Spread: 76.2bp

Embedded Call Option Value: 8.49% of par

Option-Free Yield: 5.96%

Option-Free Price: 108.94% of face amount (= 100.45 + 8.46)

	OAS Method	Option-Free	To Call on 10/15/13	To Maturity
Yield:	n/a	5.96%	6.67%	6.59%
Spread:	76.2bp	75.3bp	166.1bp	137.9bp
Modified Duration:	9.01	n/a	5.44	12.60
Risk:	9.11	n/a	5.50	12.73
Convexity:	–0.18	n/a	0.36	2.49

Note: A typical OAS analysis for a callable bond.

SOURCE: BLOOMBERG

and embedded option value are known, the price of its hypothetical underlying bullet can be determined by combining these values according to equation 3.3, which expresses the relationship among the callable-bond components. In this instance, the value of the actual callable bond, B_{cb}, is $100.45; the call option's intrinsic value, c_i, is $0.00 (since it is not currently exercisable); and the call's time value, c_t, is $8.49. Rearranging equation 3.3 to solve for the price of the underlying bullet in terms of these known values gives:

$$
\begin{aligned}
B_{ub} &= B_{cb} + (c_i + c_t) \\
&= \$100.45 + (\$0.00 + \$8.49) \\
&= \$108.94
\end{aligned}
$$

Given the callable Pacific Bell (AT&T) bond's $100.45 price and its $8.49 embedded option value, the total cost of owning a 6.625 percent Pacific Bell (AT&T) bullet bond maturing on 10/15/34 would be $108.94. In other words, the callable Pacific Bell (AT&T) bond's $100.45 price, in conjunction with the yield curve and volatility inputs to the binomial tree model, implies a $108.94 price for a bullet issue with the identical coupon and maturity. This $108.94 price, referred to as the **option-free price** of the callable bond, would be the cost of the issue without the short position in the embedded call option. Alternatively, the $8.49 option value may be viewed as the amount received by the seller of the option (the investor) from the buyer (the issuer) and represents the amount by which the hypothetical bullet bond's price was decreased to price the actual callable bond.

From its option-free price, the callable Pacific Bell (AT&T) bond's **option-free yield** may be determined. Option-free yield is simply the yield to maturity associated with the bond's option-free price and represents the yield of the underlying bullet, as implied by the model inputs and price of the callable bond. The Pacific Bell (AT&T) bond's $108.94 option-free price provides a 5.96 percent option-free yield to maturity, which represents what the yield of the callable bond would be if it were a bullet. This yield is shown under the Option-Free Yield heading in table 11.1.

In contrast, the callable bond's actual $100.45 price implies a yield to the 10/15/13 call of 6.67 percent, shown under the To Call On 10/15/13 column heading, and a yield to maturity of 6.59 percent, shown in the To Maturity column. As discussed at the end of Chapter 8, these yields are based on the assumption that interest rates remain unchanged, that is, that future interest rates are known with certainty, over the remaining life of the bond. The 5.96 percent option-free yield includes the monetary value of the embedded call, which is based on a specified level of uncertainty for future interest rates, and is viewed as the expected yield of the bond. The additional $8.49 cost associated with buying back the short call, undertaken to insure that cash flows exist until maturity, causes the overall cost of the bond to rise from $100.45 to $108.94, reducing its yield to maturity from 6.59 percent to 5.96 percent.

A similar approach may be taken with the bond's yield spread. The bond's yield to call provides a spread of 166.1bp, relative to an interpolated point on the benchmark yield curve, and its yield to maturity provides a spread of 137.9bp. However, the issue's option-free yield to maturity provides a spread of only 75.3bp. Thus, when the embedded call is taken into account, the Pacific Bell (AT&T) bond's expected yield provides a lower spread, of 75.3bp, rather than the inflated spreads associated with its conventional yields.

For those practitioners more comfortable with evaluating return on the basis of yield, rather than OAS, option-free yield and **option-free yield spread** provide convenient measures of a bond's performance that incorporate the effect of any embedded options. Consider an investor who believes that Pacific Bell (AT&T) bullet bonds maturing in October 2034 should provide a yield spread of 120bp, while a bond maturing in 10/13 (the earliest call date) should provide a yield spread of 100bp. The callable bond's yield spread—137.9bp to maturity and 166.1bp to first call—would make it appear inordinately attractive, or "cheap," to this investor, and might prompt him to purchase it. Such cheapness is often explained as extra spread provided as compensation for the presence of the call and might lead the investor to believe he was being adequately compensated for the associated risk.

However, if the investor considered the issue's 75.3bp option-free yield spread, the bond would not look nearly as attractive. Using the option-free yield spread as a gauge, he might conclude that at $100.45, this bond does not provide sufficient incremental return. He would consider purchasing it only if it provided the 120bp option-free yield spread he believes appropriate. In other words, he would buy it only if it were available at a lower price.

Option value, in addition to being measured monetarily, may also be expressed in terms of its basis-point impact on a bond's return. This impact is measured by comparing an issue's conventional yield to maturity with its option-free yield to maturity (or its yield-to-maturity spread with its option-free yield spread). In the current example, the difference between the callable Pacific Bell (AT&T) bond's yield to maturity, 6.59 percent, and its option-free yield to maturity, 5.96 percent, is 63bp. In addition to having a value of $8.49, the embedded call causes the expected yield of the bond to decrease by—and is therefore said to be "worth"—63bp. The callable bond would thus need to provide a traditional yield that is 63bp greater than the yield of a bullet with identical coupon and maturity in order to provide the same expected yield.

IN ADDITION TO providing various measures of return, the OAS methodology may be used to measure a bond's price sensitivity to changes in interest rates. This application of the analysis is concerned with quantifying the extent to which a bond's price will change in response to a shift in interest rates.

Traditional **modified duration** is a predictive measure of the expected percentage change in a bond's price in response to a 100bp shift in its yield. It is based on the issue's yield and the number, magnitude, and time to receipt of its future cash flows. Thus, if it is assumed that the Pacific Bell (AT&T) bond will be called on 10/15/14, the issue's traditional modified duration is calculated as 5.44, meaning that a 100bp change from its present yield will result in a 5.44 percent change in its $100.45 price. On the other hand, if it is assumed that the issue is not called before its 10/15/34 maturity, its duration is calculated as 12.60, indicating that it would be expected to undergo a larger 12.60 percent change in price for the same 100bp change in yield. These modified duration values are shown in the Modified Duration row in table 11.1.

Market participants concerned with forecasting or hedging against price movements for this issue would find these two price-sensitivity measures of little use, since it is unclear whether either value is appropriate. This problem is compounded by the fact that, since the issue may be called on any date between 10/15/13 and 10/15/34, its duration may assume any value between 5.44 and 12.60—a range of possible price sensitivities with an upper value 231 percent greater than the lower!

The obvious drawbacks of traditional price-sensitivity measures for nonbullet bonds are circumvented when OAS analysis is employed to measure the **effective duration** of a bond. Whereas traditional duration seeks to predict a bond's price changes based on its given price and assumed redemption date, effective duration uses actual price changes resulting from specified shifts in interest rates.

One method of measuring a bond's effective duration employs the following procedure: First, each of the rates composing the benchmark yield curve are increased, or parallel-shifted upward, by a nominal amount, such as 50bp. Second, implied spot and forward rates are recalculated. Third, holding volatility and the bond's OAS constant, a new price for the bond is calculated. The procedure is repeated using a downward parallel shift of equal magnitude. The resulting prices describe the extent to which the bond's price will change from its current value for the interest-rate shifts modeled, providing a measure of the issue's effective duration.

When a bond contains an embedded option, its effective duration is often referred to as its **OAS duration**. There are two key advantages associated with measuring a nonbullet bond's duration on an option-adjusted basis: First, by incorporating the binomial tree, the analysis takes into account the interest-rate-dependent nature of the cash flow. It does this by holding the issue's OAS constant over the specified interest-rate shifts, in effect holding constant the credit spread demanded by the market from the issuer. The behavior of the embedded option as interest rates change is thus taken into account. Second, OAS duration is calculated based on a general shift in the benchmark interest rates composing the risk-free yield curve, and so indicates the bond's price response to changes in interest rates in general rather than with respect to its own yield.

The Pacific Bell (AT&T) bond's OAS duration of 9.01 is shown in the OAS Method column of table 11.1. Based on the price changes resulting from the upward and downward shifts in the yield curve, this bond's price would be expected to change by 9.01 percent for a 100bp parallel shift. Since this issue's OAS duration is roughly midway between its 10/15/14 call-date and 10/15/34 maturity-date duration, the conclusion is that the issue's current price behavior is much like that of a bond maturing in 2024. This is further evidenced by the moderately high $8.49 embedded option value, which indicates that the model has the call in the money at many nodes on its future exercise dates.

Whereas duration describes the rate at which a bond's price changes with respect to interest rates, convexity describes how a bond's duration changes with respect to interest rates. In essence, convexity characterizes the degree to which a price increase associated with a downward shift in rates exceeds a price decrease associated with an equal upward shift in rates. As with duration, effective, or OAS, convexities for a bond may be determined by employing the model to generate explicit prices in response to controlled shifts in rates. Traditional convexity measures, 0.36 with respect to the Pacific Bell (AT&T) bond's 10/15/14 call date and 2.49 to its 10/15/34 maturity date, are shown at the bottom of the To Call on 10/15/14 and To Maturity columns. The issue's –0.18 OAS convexity is shown at the bottom of the OAS Method column. In this case, the issue's effective convexity is only a fraction of the value given by conventional means! Additional price-sensitivity measures, such as the dollar value of a one-basis-point change in rates, may also be determined on an effective, or OAS, basis.

Since the benchmark yield curve forms the basis for measuring risk-free returns in the OAS model, changes in its shape will affect the outcome of the analysis. For example, if benchmark yields were to decrease while a bullet bond's spread were held constant, its price would increase because the lower rates in the binomial tree would generate higher present values for its cash flows. If the bond were callable, lower rates would generate higher underlying bullet prices on the call date, increasing its embedded option value and causing a greater share of the prices on this date to be replaced by the lower call price. As a result, the call would undergo the price appreciation that would have otherwise been enjoyed by the bond. This effect is compounded if the exercise date of the call occurs earlier in the life of the issue, since an earlier call will capture a greater number of subsequent cash flows than a later call date. If rates continued to decline, more and more of the prices on the embedded call's exercise date will be discarded and replaced with the lower call price, driving the option deeper into the money and stalling the price appreciation of the bond.

Since its introduction in Chapter 7, the uncertainty parameter, or percent short-rate volatility, has played an important role in all aspects of OAS analysis. Because bullet bonds provide cash flows that are not interest-rate-dependent, they are unaffected by changes in volatility. In other words, no matter how much uncertainty prescribed for short rates, and regardless of the range of their possible values, the future payment stream of such bonds remains unaffected. For a given price, a bullet bond will provide the same expected return and have the same price sensitivity at all volatility levels.

Nonbullet bonds, on the other hand, have returns that are dependent on the level of uncertainty specified for the short rates. For example, an increase in volatility will generate a wider range of short rates in the model, producing a wider range of prices for the underlying instrument on an option's exercise date. Nodes previously in the money will be driven deeper in the money, causing option value to increase at these nodes. If assumed that all nodes previously out of the money remain out of the money after volatility is increased (as opposed to assuming that some of these nodes are driven in the money), their zero option values remain unchanged.

As a result, the expected payout of the option will increase if volatility is increased. Callable-bond prices, which reflect the value of the short embedded call, suffer from increases in volatility; put-bond prices, which include the value of the long embedded put, benefit from such increases.

CHAPTER 12

ESTIMATING FAIR VALUE

THUS FAR, THE FOCUS has been on using option-adjusted spread (OAS) analysis as a tool for measuring the incremental return of bonds with significantly different structures, that is, of bonds with and without embedded options. The emphasis has been on the determination of an OAS or option-free yield spread, given the bond's price, a risk-free benchmark volatility (uncertainty) assumption, and a risk-free benchmark yield curve. It was also stated that though the spread resulting from such an analysis could be thought of as a pure credit spread, the value itself conveys little information about whether the underlying bond is appropriately valued, forcing potential investors to decide for themselves whether the incremental return provides sufficient compensation for the bond's risks.

The process of judging whether a bond—or any security—is appropriately valued is an important and often difficult task for market professionals. In the fixed-income arena, investors, traders, and marketers continually evaluate the attractiveness of bonds by weighing their expected returns against their perceived risks. Return measures, as explained earlier, range from yields and yield spreads to option-adjusted spreads and option-free yields. Investors are typically exposed to varying degrees of credit, liquidity, sector, interest-rate, and reinvestment risk, among others. The extent of such risks may generally be ascertained by researching the issuer's credit stance, relevant company and industry news, and the bond's structure, including any provisions for early principal redemption.

Although these methods help to quantify a given bond's risk and return attributes, they do not tell whether the return it provides is appropriate to its risks. *An OAS value is only useful as a means of comparing bonds.* To make this determination, one needs to compare the bond's return with the returns provided by other issues within its sector. If the given bond's return is equivalent to or otherwise in agreement with the returns provided by similar bonds, then conclusively the issue is appropriately valued. In a sense, OAS levels the playing field across different structures so that bonds in similar sectors can be compared. Bonds of similar creditworthiness, similar industry, and similar maturities should have similar OAS values. If not, the investor should ask, "Why not?"

More often than not, comparisons like the one described above are conducted on a yield basis. As seen earlier, this approach is severely limited by unrealistic assumptions in yield calculations including redemption and reinvestment assumptions. An alternative approach is to calculate the OAS values for each of the similar bonds sampled and use their consensus average as a gauge by which to judge the OAS of the bond in question. Though this approach is acceptable in cases where a sufficient number of similarly structured bonds are priced, it is of little help in cases where similar structures either do not exist or are inadequately priced. In addition, because many model implementations of OAS analysis employ a single constant spread to an underlying benchmark curve, they cannot incorporate the manner in which credit spreads vary with maturity, making it difficult to use credit-spread observations on somewhat dissimilar bonds in the analysis.

It is possible, however, to alter the customary OAS analysis to avoid the various difficulties outlined in the previous paragraph and focus on whether a bond is appropriately valued. Such an analysis is referred to as **theoretical fair-value analysis**, the objective of which is to calculate the theoretical fair price for a selected bond.

The full analysis can be thought of as being conducted in three stages:

I Screening and organizing market pricing data
II Solving for sector, yield-curve, and volatility attributes
III Estimating the theoretical fair value of the bond being considered

Note that the first two stages analyze the broad market sector, while only the last focuses on the bond itself. As shall be shown, the bulk of the work in deriving a bond's fair value is done in stages I and II.

The most significant distinction between customary OAS and fair-value analysis is that the latter replaces the risk-free interest-rate environment with the interest-rate environment of the market sector of which the bond under consideration is a part (that is, "change the curve"). Specifically, fair-value analysis replaces the risk-free benchmark yield curve with the yield curve for the bond's sector, and risk-free interest-rate volatility with the interest-rate volatility of the bond's sector. The logic at work here is that whereas customary OAS analysis seeks to quantify the expected incremental return of a bond against the backdrop of risk-free market conditions, fair-value analysis seeks to quantify a theoretical value for the bond based on the return attributes of bonds in its own sector.

By far the most challenging task faced by those who conduct fair-value analyses is determining the structure of the sector interest-rate environment. The other aspects of the analysis are almost trivial by comparison. The difficulty associated with determining the yield curve and volatility that "best" price the bonds in a given sector is chiefly due to the wide variation in bond structures encountered in, and often-incomplete pricing information available from, the market. As a result, serious practitioners resort to the use of optimization routines to identify the yield curve/volatility combination that best represents a given sector.

The following paragraphs describe one possible method of conducting a fair-value analysis, with the important understanding that other methods are equally valid. The aim here is not to describe all possible computation methods but to illustrate underlying principles. In reality, methodologies should be selected on the basis of how well their predictions correlate with market observations.

STAGE I

Screening and Organizing Market Pricing Data

1 Get universe of well-priced bonds. The construction of an accurate **sector yield curve** is of critical importance to fair-value analysis. For this reason, it is essential to base the analysis on accurate market data. The first step, therefore, is to identify those issues within the universe of bonds traded in a particular market, such as U.S. corporates, for which consensus market prices are available and disregard the rest. This insures that only accurate market data are used in the computations.

2 Bucket by industry. It is important to segment the market in a way that gathers together securities with broadly similar risk profiles; the resulting yield curve will thus describe returns as a function of maturity, with other factors, such as credit and sector risk, effectively held constant. Segregating the consensus-priced issues identified in step 1 by industry sector, such as industrial, utility, or finance, insures that sector-specific economic and event risks are the same for all issues. This effectively holds the risk component constant for the group.

3 Bucket by credit rating. Issues are further sorted by credit rating, creating a credit ladder within each industry group. This insures that all issues within each sector grouping have similar economic, event, and credit risks.

STAGE II

Solving for Sector Yield-Curve and Volatility Attributes

4 Separate bullets and callables. Once the broad markets are segmented into sectors with homogeneous risks, bonds within a given sector are further divided into two groups: those with embedded options and those without.

5 Build sector curve of bullets. The bullet bonds are used to construct the first estimation of the sector yield curve by plotting their yields (to maturity) against their maturities. The resulting curve, by definition, is option-free.

6 Calculate full term structure. The sector's term structure of interest rates (implied spot and forward rates) is determined, based on the yield-curve estimation made in step 5.

7 Choose starting volatility. An estimate of the sector interest-rate volatility rate is made. (This may be chosen from the **swaptions** market.)

8 Combine curve and volatility. An interest-rate model is built using the term structure determined in step 6 and the volatility estimate from step 7.

9 Calculate OAS for all bonds. The OAS of each bond in the sector—bullet and nonbullet—is calculated relative to the interest-rate model constructed in step 8. Note that these OAS values are relative to the sector curve, not the benchmark curve.

10 Measure fit of the model to sample population. An average value for the spreads determined in step 9 is calculated. Since it is important to capture the magnitude of OAS values that may be negative, the absolute values or squares of the OAS values—rather than the values themselves—are computed, summed, and averaged.

11 Reiterate and optimize the model. The average spread magnitude computed in step 10 can be thought of as an indication of the deviation of the modeled interest-rate environment, which is specified, versus the real world, which we are trying to model. The best model for the sector is the one that produces a minimum average spread in step 10. Since the yield curve and volatility parameters completely define the modeled environment, changes in these parameters will generate a new set of spreads and, therefore, a new average spread. Specifically, changes in the yield-curve parameter will affect the OAS of all bonds, while changes in the volatility parameter will affect the OAS of nonbullet bonds only. The optimization routine employs numerical calculation methods designed to identify the combination of yield curve and volatility values that minimizes the sector's average spread. The yield curve and volatility values that result from the optimization calculations are defined as the sector **option-free yield curve** and the **sector implied volatility**.

STAGE III

Estimating the Theoretical Fair Value of a Bond

12 Price bond with model. Once the sector interest-rate environment is described and quantified in terms of the sector yield curve and volatility, the theoretical fair value of any bond in the sector may be calculated. This is done by instructing the OAS model to accept as input a spread to the sector curve and a sector volatility and to solve for a price. In most instances, the specified spread is zero, which causes the bond's cash flows to be present-valued (in the manner discussed in Chapters 9 and 10) using the sector's unaltered interest-rate environment. Since the curve and volatility composing this environment were derived from the prices and returns of many bonds in the sector, the fair value of a bond can be thought of as the value of the security implied by the returns of other similarly rated issues in the bond's sector.

The credit quality of bond issuers can be thought of as describing a roughly continuous scale of riskiness, with issuers along the scale grouped into categories defined by rating agencies. Within each category, therefore, there exists a spectrum of riskiness. It is important to bear in mind that the option-free yield curve and the sector volatility used in the fair-value analysis are derived from the returns of bonds distributed over the credit spectrum within the sector; they therefore represent *average* values for the sector as a whole. A bond whose fair value is derived from a zero spread, therefore, is assumed to have risks equivalent to the average for the sector. In some instances, the perceived risks of a particular issuer—and hence the return demanded of its bonds by the market—will differ from the average values for the sector as a whole. For these issuers, it is customary to specify an adjustment in the form of a spread to the underlying sector rates to compensate for the incremental risk.

This incremental spread is employed in precisely the same manner as the option-adjusted spread discussed in Chapters 9 and 10: a positive value raises the rates in the model and is typically specified for an issue perceived to carry greater-than-average credit risk. The higher rates generate a fair value that is lower than it would have been without the credit adjustment. Similarly, a negative spread lowers rates in the model and is used when an issue is thought to possess less-than-average credit risk and generates a fair value that is higher than it otherwise would be.

Once the theoretical fair value of a bond is determined, including any credit-spread adjustment, it may be used as a benchmark value against which the attractiveness of an observed price can be gauged. In general, the fair value may be thought of as a threshold value: If its observed price is greater than the fair value, a bond is considered overvalued; if the observed price is lower than the fair value, it is considered undervalued. If the observed market price of a security is equivalent to the fair value, it is considered appropriately valued. One must be careful that no developments, such as takeovers, earnings reports, or legislation, are at work that would account for significant differences between a bond's market price and the fair value.

Consider the Pacific Bell (AT&T) 6.625 percent 10/15/34 bonds. This bond's description, including a call provision, is shown in table 2.3. As a telecommunications company, Pacific Bell (AT&T) is considered a communications entity and, under the structure outlined above, would be grouped with other telephone bonds. Its credit quality is rated A2 by Moody's Investors Service and A by Standard & Poor's Corp. The fair value of this bond is thus derived from the returns evident in the market for all A telephone bonds.

TABLE 12.1 contains a typical fair-value analysis for this bond, showing the A telephone-bond option-free yield curve and the sector implied volatility of 9.75 percent.

In this example, the binomial model underlying the OAS calcu-

TABLE 12.1

Theoretical Fair-Value Analysis

Pacific Bell (AT&T) CUSIP: 694032AX1
6.625% Bond Priced @ 100.45

INPUTS	
Settlement Date:	12/20/06
Sector Implied Volatility:	9.75%
Input Spread Adjustment:	0.0bp

Term	Yield (%)
3 mo	5.248
6 mo	5.284
1 yr	5.389
2 yr	5.270
3 yr	5.304
4 yr	5.430
5 yr	5.521
7 yr	5.589
10 yr	5.825
15 yr	6.317
20 yr	6.357
25 yr	6.393
30 yr	6.308

OUTPUTS OF LOGNORMAL MODEL	
Output Fair Value:	99.04% of par

ANALYSIS OF OUTPUT	
Actual Price:	100.45% of face amount
Output Fair Value:	99.04% of face amount
Price Difference:	–0.49% of face amount (= 99.04 – 100.45)
Actual Composite Rating:	A
Implied Rating:	A

Note: A fair-value analysis for a bond whose actual and implied ratings agree.

SOURCE: BLOOMBERG

lations derives spot and forward rates from the A telephone-sector curve, applies the annualized short-rate sector volatility rate of 9.75 percent to the resulting term structure *(see Chapters 5 and 7)*, and calibrates the resulting interest-rate model to recover a price of par for the theoretical par-coupon bonds composing the given curve *(see Chapter 8)*. Once the interest-rate model is in place, the Pacific Bell (AT&T) bond is priced by specifying a zero-spread to the A telephone short rates composing the binomial tree. At those nodes where the modeled price exceeds the embedded call's strike price, the model price is replaced by the lower call price *(see Chapter 10)*. The resulting present value represents the Pacific Bell (AT&T) bond's theoretical fair value, 99.04, shown as the Output Fair Value in the table.

The actual price given in the table for this bond is 100.45. This is 0.49 points higher than its fair value, which was determined without any credit-adjustment spread. This small price difference suggests that the Pacific Bell (AT&T) issue is currently priced to trade slightly better than an average A telephone credit.

Deviations between a bond's fair value and its market price imply that the market perceives the credit risk of the issuer to be different from that of the broad rating class. Under these circumstances, it is useful to identify the credit rating implied by the market price. When a full complement of yield curves for each rating level within an industry sector exists, the sequential credit domains produce a "ladder" of yield curves arranged in order of increasing or decreasing credit risk. If each of these curves is used to price the bond, a series of model prices is generated, each associated with a particular credit level within the industry. The credit rating whose curve generates the model price closest to the bond's observed price is referred to as the bond's **implied credit rating**.

This type of fair-value modeling allows practitioners to measure how a particular bond is priced relative to the peer group of similar issuers' bonds. The reader should be aware that some issuers, due to extraneous circumstances, may always price rich or cheap relative to the peer group. Further, reasons for this may include limited liquidity, particular financial conditions, or other issuer idiosyncrasies. For example, tobacco always trades cheap as do airlines.

CONCLUSION

Building a Better OAS

THIS BOOK EXPLAINS a traditional approach to solving for the option-adjusted spread of a bond: how an investor can identify the value inherent in the cash flows and embedded options relative to market reference levels. Underlying the method is the theory that a bond can be described as a portfolio of zero-coupon strips (the cash flows) and interest-rate options (the calls and/or puts). The incremental yield an investor receives on the bond above benchmark alternatives is a combination of interest premium and option premium. Through appropriate modeling techniques, one can discretely value the option components and thus clarify the incremental spread paid on the cash flows versus benchmark.

It has been more than ten years since this book first went to press, and it is no slight understatement to say that computational methods have advanced since then. From the quantitative side, more advanced methods of option valuation became available that better reconcile to recent historical observations. Computationally, huge "big iron mainframes" have given way to clustered server farms with massively parallel architectures, obliterating previous calculation speeds by many orders of magnitude. Data of rates and volatility that were once guarded secrets are now readily available commodities.

As a result of such progress, an investor can now, for a price, employ a variety of "upgrades" to traditional OAS analysis, and apply OAS models to a broad selection of bond types. In keeping with the general theme of the book, this chapter will take a light look at some evolutions since the first publishing.

Reference Curves

When OAS analysis first gained traction in the markets as a better valuation tool, models were generally driven by the relevant sovereign bond curve, for example, U.S. Treasuries, English Gilts, or German Bunds. The logic was simple: an investor could buy the risky bond, or the investor could buy the "riskless benchmark." OAS analysis would give a more accurate indication of the incremental spread of the risky bond *relative* to the benchmark curve on a "per cash flow" basis.

But these "government" curves, built with bonds, contain problematic elements from an analytic point of view. First is the idea that when actual securities are used to build a curve, they do not have the same time to maturity as the days go by. For example, if the U.S. Treasury 2-year note is used for the 2-year point of the curve, after two weeks the bond has moved almost 2 percent of its total time to maturity. Yield curves built with bonds exhibit "shrinkage" as the bonds roll down the curve. And the changes in yield seen on these bonds are affected by this behavior—even if market conditions do not change, the bonds should adjust yield by simply moving closer to a lower nominal point on the curve. This is why one hears the term *constant maturity* used in many fixed-income contexts—we need to be able to study the term structure of rates with consistent relative time.

Another problem with using curves built with benchmark bonds is the influence of "cost of carry." In order to place an asset on a typical balance sheet, there will be an associated liability (for every use of funds, there is a source of funds). And while the fixed-income asset generates interest income, the associated liability (borrowing) will generate interest expense. The difference between interest income and interest expense is known as "cost of carry." Carry, as it is commonly known, significantly affects decisions of bond traders—especially short sellers—and the associated economic effects can create aberrations in the yield curve when supply and demand is imbalanced.

The relation of the reference curve to the assets being valued is another sticky wicket. Is it really appropriate to benchmark a corporate bond versus an issuer that can literally print money? This is a question of "basis," the natural difference between two different investment classes, and whether they are consistently correlated for comparative purposes.

For OAS analysis purposes, most regular practitioners have left the government curves behind in favor of the interest-rate swap curve to overcome many issues like this. Interest-rate swaps are very useful and very common derivatives used to transfer fixed-rate and floating-rate risk. Primarily, they harness the concept that a term interest rate is the geometric average of a series of short-term rates over the same period.

Mathematically, if given a term structure of rates, one can solve to find a fixed coupon that generates the same economic value as the expected level of discrete short rates during that period. If they are economically equivalent, then someone will be willing to swap them, because they believe that balance will soon change. Most swap rates in major currencies simply quote a fixed rate for a given term that is exchanged versus a short-term floating rate, usually either a three-month or six-month rate that resets quarterly or semiannually. Engaging in an interest-rate swap is equivalent to being long a fixed-rate bond and short a floating-rate bond, or vice versa.

For example, imagine a treasurer at a small bank who borrows money by issuing three-month deposits and lends money by making thirty-year fixed-rate mortgages. This treasurer has significant exposure (rate risk) to rising short-term rates. An interest-rate swap can neutralize this risk by allowing the treasurer to pay fixed interest rates to a swap counterparty for a given term and receive floating-rate payments from the swap counterparty with which to pay the depositors. Net, the treasurer is now paying fixed rates on the deposits and is no longer exposed to rising short-term rates.

Interest-rate swaps are well quoted and quite liquid in all major currencies now, although that was not true ten years ago. Swaps are generally exchanging fixed rates versus a standard short-term benchmark—such as the London interbank offered rate (Libor), a set of short-term rates published every day by the British Bankers Association—where banks are making loans to high-credit financial institutions and corporations. (Libor rates represent an average level where a nondomestic bank, free of regulatory or political persuasion, will lend to another highly rated financial institution. Libor lending is typically considered a AA credit level.) Swap contracts are quoted daily to standard maturities, or tenors. Typical swap contracts rarely involve the exchange of a principal amount; these contracts are actually trading rate differentials, so swaps do not appear on the balance sheet and they have no cost of carry. Furthermore, *options* on swap contracts are also very liquid and well quoted in most major currencies, thus supplying a decent estimation of forward-looking volatility expectations. When running OAS valuation, interest-rate swaps provide a significantly better benchmark curve. Swap curves provide a set of rates that represent the efficient frontier between fixed and floating rates; the rates are of constant maturity from day to day, are much more correlated to corporate borrowing levels, and are relatively free of effects from cost of carry. When given the option, choose the swap curve as a better reference curve.

So what is better than swaps for a reference curve? Determining fair value is best done when the reference curve for benchmarking is very closely related to the bond being valued. Another approach to curve selection is to use a credit curve, ideally one to which the bond has some "belonging." For instance, if one wishes to value a bond with a BBB credit rating, why not use an option-free BBB credit curve? The advantage here is that one will see how the spread of the bond, after option adjustment (of course!), compares to bonds of similar credit quality. If the bond offers a much lower OAS, one might consider its price relatively rich to the peer group of bonds contained in the credit curve. In the U.S. agency markets, most bonds currently being issued are callable and are usually valued on an OAS basis. The curves used in those situations are usually built from bonds from the *same issuer*—thus, if one wishes to value a bond from Fannie Mae, one can get very accurate valuations calculating the OAS relative to a collection (curve) of

Fannie Mae bonds. A fair price for the bond is that which gives a zero OAS to the Fannie Mae curve. If the OAS is zero, then the collection of cash flows (the bond) are priced at no advantage or disadvantage relative to other Fannie Mae rates in the marketplace. A positive OAS value suggests that the price of the bond is giving a yield advantage relative to the reference curve levels—the bond is cheap. A negative value suggests the bond price is a bit expensive, or "rich," to the market.

Typically, unless one examines an issuer with a relatively large number of well-priced bonds, a good issuer-specific curve is not available. But having an "issuer curve" does represent a best-case scenario where very accurate pricing can be derived.

Adjusting Curves

The mathematics of most OAS programs is much more elaborate that anything presented in this book. Part of the reason for this is to make a readable book for the layman; part is that mathematicians and programmers have their own interesting bag of tricks for speeding calculations and avoiding unpleasant scenarios (like negative interest rates). Building curves with bonds, like the Treasury curve or a typical credit curve, is inherently problematic. Behind the computational curtain, be aware that almost all the math is done with zero-coupon curves, also known as "spot curves." These sets of rates represent yields without intermittent cash flows. Generally, OAS programs will show curve rates in their conventional expression, maybe semiannual or annual coupon rates. The necessary conversions are done for you behind the scenes, but the user generally needs to check the rates versus market levels, which are always seen in "street convention" basis. For example, U.S. dollar swap rates are quoted as a semiannual 30/360-day basis. This is not what the program actually uses, but we don't care about that part; we need to know that the rates being used match the current market. Now, if using a curve built on bonds, one knows from the above discussion that this gets problematic; the bonds will have mismatches with respect to time where the actual time to maturity does not match the time value for the curve, and even worse, most of the bonds will not price at par. If the bonds are not priced at par, then their duration and convexity will not show consistent change relative to other bonds on the curve. This can create problems in the calculation of OAS and effective duration and convexity relative to curve shifts. When evaluating OAS models, look to see if these factors can be accommodated. One typical solution involves on-the-fly creation of synthetic par-coupon curve points with zero OAS and appropriate maturities.

Interest Rate Models and Option Valuation

Because OAS is basically a statistical process involving valuation over a large number of "what if" scenarios, quantitative analysts tend to become quite interested in the methods of modeling interest-rate paths and option valuation. Some models tend toward generating paths as a binomial or trinomial process, which basically suggests that the "wending way" of interest rates is forked like the branches of a tree, and at each fork, the rates may move in two or three new paths, which become part of the statistical evaluation. The explanations in the body of this book examine a binomial process. More recently, with the advent of higher computer processing capacity, better OAS applications can use **stochastic** modeling, such as Monte Carlo techniques, to generate scenarios. (Think of *stochastic* as "possessing a random or chaotic characteristic," like the real world. Risk managers tend to prefer such models, but the computational requirements are significantly higher.) But an OAS model cannot just let the term structure of interest rates fly randomly around the room. Short-term rates and long-term rates typically move in some form of related, continuous fashion. And it is extremely rare for rates to go negative (but not impossible). This implies that an optimal model will generate a realistic distribution of possible outcomes, and that the sets of rates and volatilities will somewhat emulate what we think could happen in the real world. Unquestionably, the quality of the interest-rate model and the scenario generation it provides directly determines the worthiness of the statistical results. With increased computing power, many higher-order OAS models are now providing "two-factor" term structure interest-rate models. Such models effectively allow a certain independence between short rates and longer-term rates as scenarios are generated for valuation trials. Older model structures typically generated scenarios where short rates varied and longer rates were completely dependent on the change in short rates. New two-factor models remove that "convenience to computation" and the result is a more realistic evolution of term structure.

The interest-rate model also includes the volatility landscape used for valuation of the embedded options. Volatility values come in two major flavors: historical and implied. **Historical volatility** simply looks back at the variance of price of a series and puts a numerical value on how much variance has been observed, usually by describing the standard deviation. While it is always useful to look back at historical behavior of prices, most investors are even more interested in future expectations. More useful to financial-markets players is **implied volatility**. Implied volatility compares observed prices of options on an instrument to the price of the instrument itself. And using an option valuation method (Black-Scholes, Hull-White, and others), one can calculate how much volatility the market expects for the underlying instrument—that is, what does the market price of the option imply for volatility?

Implied volatilities are numerical coefficients that describe how much uncertainty surrounds the future value of a number—be that number a stock price, an index, or maybe an interest rate. Higher volatility suggests a wider set of possible future values and greater uncertainty. Lower volatility is the opposite—less uncertainty of an object's value in the future. If volatility increases, a long position in options will increase in value. (**Long an option**: pay a fee [premium] for the right, but not the obligation, to "do unto others" at a predetermined price. **Short an option**: get paid a premium, but they can "do unto you.") Option traders love volatility, and valuing any options—like those embedded in callable bonds—requires information on volatility from the marketplace so we can value the options in callable bonds.

To make things more interesting, implied volatility for a given security or instrument has its own special structure. Most options markets offer a series of contracts over an extended time horizon with a variety of available strike prices. For instance, a given security might be trading at a price of 75. Perhaps one could buy options for exercise three months hence, six months hence, one year hence, and so forth. And, for each of these forward dates, the market offers different "strike prices," the levels at which the owner can exercise his right to buy or sell. For each exercise date in the future, one might see contracts for exercise at 70, 72.5, 75, 77.5 and 80. Note that within each series for a given exercise date, one contract of the series has a strike equal to the current or expected price of the underlying instrument. This contract is called the "at the money" contract and it represents a very efficient member of the options series, with highest volume and most readily available pricing. Notably, as one moves across available strikes, the implied volatility from the various pricing exhibits changing levels for similar dates. This structure of volatility levels is known as "skew," or sometimes "a smile." Some studies explain skew with respect to supply and demand; others ascribe it to imperfection in pricing models. When these relative levels of implied volatility for various strikes are mapped across the exercise dates out over the time horizon, a "surface map" of the term structure of volatility is defined. This map of volatility levels is described three-dimensionally over axes of time, strike level, and volatility, and is commonly called a "volatility surface" or "volatility cube." When this level of volatility information is available, one can derive more accurate option valuation. Most OAS models do not do this; they are typically run based on a single volatility value, or possibly a term structure of at-the-money volatilities. Remember that the quality of the OAS valuation is very dependent on option valuation.

Good volatility data are becoming fairly available from the options market on swaps, contracts known as "swaptions." Some people find swaps a bit confusing at first, but think of swaps as simply "converter" tools that change fixed-rate exposure to floating-rate exposure or vice versa. If one held a fixed-rate bond and suddenly wished it to be a floater, the swap would provide that conversion. By adding a swap contract to the trade, the bondholder can effectively pay away the fixed coupons of the bond and receive floating coupons from the swap counterparty. Presto! The bondholder now has floating risk, instead. (Many refer to this combination of fixed-rate bond and swap contract as a "synthetic floater.") Corporate treasurers use this technique quite frequently when they issue fixed-rate bonds but would rather have a floating-rate liability. The bond market usually has a better appetite for fixed-coupon issues, so a corporate treasurer will probably get a better rate. Additionally, the underwriting dealer is typically glad to provide a big swap contract along with an underwriting (*would you like fries with that?*). Given that a swap contract is a financial tool for removing fixed-rate exposure, it is not a big jump to conceptualize that a swaption is a tool offering "the right, but not the obligation" to change interest-rate exposure. The treasurer who issued a callable bond is long the right, at some future date, to change the interest-rate exposure from an existing fixed level (the coupon on the bond). This is why swaptions volatility is the typical input for fixed-income option valuation.

Things to Keep in Mind

First, always remember that OAS analysis is a *relative* measuring tool. Just saying that a bond has an OAS of a given value does not mean much. OAS analysis is best used for comparing one security to another or to a peer group. The main mission of OAS analysis is to isolate the yield premium from the option premium, allowing comparison across bullets, callables, and putables.

Also, it is perfectly appropriate to measure bullets alone with OAS analysis, for this valuation technique properly values cash flows relative to the time value of money expressed across the yield curve. This is a fundamental flaw behind traditional yield analysis solved by OAS methods. OAS on a bullet bond is analogous to the Z-spread.

OAS analysis is also applied to portfolios in aggregate; however, averaging is not appropriate. The entire portfolio must be reduced to its constituent cash flows and embedded options, then OAS modeling is applied. Portfolio OAS analysis can be useful when considering changes to the constituent bonds and the effect on overall spread. It is also useful to see how different portfolios may change valuation or risk characteristics with overall curve shifts or various spread shocks.

Finally, remember that results of different models are not comparable. Many experienced practitioners suggest that success lies in using one model consistently, and knowing the shortcomings of the model, then closing your eyes and jumping.

Other Securities

While most of the book has treated bonds fairly generically with almost all the examples being based on U.S. corporates, most OAS models usually work well for other types of bonds, too.

◆ Municipal bonds are regularly priced with OAS analysis using municipal curves such as a AAA-rated composite general obligation curve, or possibly a state-specific curve. Interesting questions arise regarding appropriate volatilities (or a percentage thereof). Typical approaches seek the volatilities that move observed callable prices to equivalent OAS levels with liquid bullet bonds.

◆ U.S. government agency bond traders use OAS analysis every day when valuing both new issuance and secondary-market prices. Large liquid bullet issues in this market provide very reliable reference curves, thus allowing a buyer to price a bond's cash flows fairly to the issuer's own rate levels.

◆ Convertible bonds can also be priced with OAS models, but a new twist is introduced by the need to simultaneously model both fixed-income options and equity options.

◆ Mortgage-backed and asset-backed securities markets may well be the largest user groups of OAS techniques. These securities have complex and uncertain cash-flow patterns for principal and interest that make standard yield to maturity almost obsolete. The option of a home mortgage holder to pay principal early means these securities are heavily laden with short call positions for the bond purchaser. Quality of OAS models for this sector is determined by prepayment modeling for cash-flow generation, good volatility inputs with skew adjustment, and a multifactor interest-rate model.

GLOSSARY

American option. An option that may be exercised over a time period that begins sometime before, and terminates on, the option expiration date. See **European option**.

arbitrage-free binomial tree of risk-free short rates. See **lognormal model**.

at-the-money option. An option whose strike price is equal or close to the underlying security's current market price.

benchmark yield curve. The yield curve described by benchmark, or risk-free, notes and bonds. In the United States, the most recently issued Treasury bills, notes, and bonds are considered benchmark issues.

Bermudian option. With regards to fixed-income securities, any embedded option whereby the bondholder has sold the issuer the right to repurchase the bond back from the investor, on interest payment dates only, from the time that the bond is first callable until its maturity date.

binomial distribution. A probability distribution created by the results of a random process for which there are only two possible, mutually exclusive outcomes.

binomial process. A sequencing of events where only two possible outcomes develop from a preceding event.

bullet bond. A bond with a simple cash-flow structure that provides coupon, or interest, payments at regular intervals over the life of the issue and repays the full principal amount to investors at maturity.

callable bond. A bond containing a provision that allows the issuer to retire the debt before the scheduled maturity.

call option. An option contract in which the option buyer acquires the right, but not the obligation, to buy a prescribed amount of an underlying security from the option seller at a specified price during a specific exercise period.

cheap security. A security whose expected return is greater than that provided by issues with similar risks and is therefore considered undervalued. See **rich security**.

continuously callable bonds. A class of callable bonds that become eligible to be called sometime before maturity and remain callable until maturity. Continuous call features are usually modeled as **American call options**.

convexity. A measure of the extent to which a bond's **duration** changes with its yield. *Positively convex* bonds, such as bullet and put bonds, have prices that rise more for a downward change in yield than they fall for an equal upward change. *Negatively convex* bonds, such as callable bonds, have prices that rise less for a downward yield change than they fall for an equal upward change. Mathematically, the convexity (CVX) of a bond with h cash flows, each with a unique time until payment t_j and a present value P_j, m compounding periods per year, yield y, and a total present value (price plus accrued interest) of P, is given as:

$$CVX = \frac{1}{(1 + y/m)^2} \times \sum_{j=1}^{h} \frac{(j \times (j+1) \times P_j)}{(m^2 \times P)}$$

The change in a bond's price for a given change in yield, due to its convexity, is given by:

$$\frac{\Delta P}{P} = 0.5 \times (\Delta y) 2 \times CVX \times 100$$

discretely callable bonds. A class of bonds that are eligible to be called only on single dates or on a series of specific dates, such as coupon dates. Single-date discrete call features are usually modeled as **European call options**, whereas multiple-date discrete calls are modeled as **American calls** with discrete exercise dates.

duration (effective). A type of modified duration that is solved for from observed changes in a bond's price due to known interest-rate shifts, rather than from price-yield mathematics.

duration (Macaulay). A measure of a bond's price volatility, devised by Frederick Macaulay in 1938. Macaulay duration is the present-value-weighted time to receipt of a bond's cash flows, in essence describing the average length of time for a dollar to be paid to a bondholder. This measure acts as a proportionality factor that relates a percentage change in the price of a bond to a percentage change in its yield. Mathematically, the Macaulay duration ($D_{macaulay}$) of a bond with h cash flows, each with a unique time until payment t_j and a present value P_j, m compounding periods per year, yield y, and a total present value (price plus accrued interest) of P, is given as:

$$D_{macaulay} = \sum_{j=1}^{h} \frac{(P_j \times t_j)}{P}$$

The Macaulay-duration-predicted price change resulting from a specified yield change is given by:

$$\frac{\Delta P}{P} = -D_{macaulay} \times \frac{\Delta y}{(1 + y/m)}$$

duration (modified). Also referred to as *adjusted* duration, a measure of a bond's percentage change in price for a given absolute change in its yield. Mathematically, modified duration is given as:

$$D_{modified} = D_{macaulay} \times \frac{1}{(1 + y/m)}$$

The modified-duration-predicted price change from a specified absolute yield change is given by:

$$\frac{\Delta P}{P} = -D_{modified} \times \Delta y$$

For positively convex bonds, modified duration underestimates price gains and overestimates price losses; it overestimates price gains and underestimates price losses for negatively convex bonds.

duration (option-adjusted spread). A type of effective duration determined by measuring the change in price of a bond caused by perturbing the term structure of interest rates in a given manner (such as a parallel yield-curve shift) and holding the assumed volatility and the OAS of the bond constant.

embedded option. A hypothetical put or call option that models the early-principal-redemption provision of a nonbullet bond.

European option. An option that may be exercised only on its expiration date. See **American option**.

exercise price. The price at which an option holder has the right to buy (in a call option) or sell (in a put option) the underlying security.

expiration date. The date on which the provisions of an option contract cease to be in effect.

historical volatility. See **volatility**.

hypothetical options. See **embedded option**.

implied benchmark forward rate. A break-even interest rate for a future (forward) time period that is solved for from implied benchmark spot rates.

implied benchmark spot rate. An interest rate, solved for from benchmark bond yields, that accurately prices a payment from any benchmark bond occurring on a particular future date. Such rates are sometimes referred to as **theoretical zero-coupon rates**.

implied credit rating. The credit rating of a class of bonds whose yield curve generates a price for a given bond that is in closest agreement with its observed market price.

implied spot curve. A curve generated by plotting spot rates versus their maturities.

implied volatility. See **volatility**.

incremental return. The portion of a bond's return that exceeds that provided by otherwise similar risk-free securities.

in-the-money option. An option that possesses intrinsic value. A call option is in the money when it is exercisable and the price of the underlying security is greater than the call's strike price; a put option is in the money when it is exercisable and the price of the underlying security is lower than the put's strike price.

intrinsic value. A measure of the profitability of exercising an option immediately; the difference between the option's strike price and the current market price of the underlying instrument. In-the-money options have intrinsic value; at-the-money options have little or no intrinsic value; out-of-the-money options have no intrinsic value. See **time value**.

lognormal model. A fixed-income option model that generates interest rates that are lognormally distributed—that is, rates whose logarithms describe a normal distribution. A lognormal binomial interest-rate model generates two mutually exclusive outcomes for an interest rate from any node; the distribution of rates from all nodes in a given time period is lognormally distributed.

long an option. Pay a fee (premium) for the right, but not the obligation, to exercise a transaction at a predetermined price.

nonbullet bond. A bond containing provisions allowing principal repayment, in whole or in part, before the stated maturity.

option. A contract that gives the buyer the right, but not the obligation, to buy from, or sell to, the option seller a prescribed amount of an underlying instrument at a specified price during a specific exercise period. See **call option** and **put option**.

option-adjusted spread (OAS). The constant basis-point spread that must be applied to the rates in a fixed-income option model to recover the price of the bond being analyzed. When the analysis is conducted using risk-free rates, the OAS is viewed as the incremental return of the bond. True adjustments to this spread occur only when the bond contains an embedded option.

option-adjusted spread (OAS) analysis. A financial-analysis method that analyzes the impact of any options embedded in a bond's structure and measures the issue's expected incremental return.

option-free price. The price of a bond after adjusting for the value of any embedded options. In callable bonds, the option-free price is the sum of the bond price and the value of its embedded option; in putable bonds, it is the bond price less the embedded option's value. See **option-free yield**.

option-free yield. The yield to maturity associated with a bond's option-free price. This is the yield a bond would have if it were a bullet. See **option-free price**.

option-free yield curve. A curve built from option-free yields.

option-free yield spread. The yield spread associated with a bond's option-free yield to maturity.

option premium. The amount paid to purchase, or received from the sale of, an option.

option strike price. See **exercise price**.

option value. The worth of an option at a particular point in time, as computed by an option-valuation model.

option-valuation models. The broad class of financial analysis tools designed to estimate the value of options.

out-of-the-money option. An option that possesses no intrinsic value. A call option is out of the money when the price of the underlying security is less than the call's strike; a put option is out of the money when the price of the underlying is greater than the put's strike.

overhedged. A condition in which the risk exposure of a hedge position exceeds that of the primary position being hedged.

par. When an instrument is trading at 100 percent of face value. Also used to reference the total face value of a quantity of bonds.

percent volatility of short rates. The relative uncertainty of future prices of an instrument. It represents an annualized standard deviation of daily change in price.

price sensitivity. The extent to which a bond's price changes when a factor to which its price is linked, such as interest rates, changes.

putable bond. A bond that contains a provision that allows the bondholder to receive the principal before the scheduled maturity.

put option. An option contract in which the option buyer acquires the right, but not the obligation, to sell a prescribed amount of an underlying security to the option seller at a specified price during a specific exercise period.

rich security. A security whose expected return is less than that provided by issues with similar risks and is therefore considered overvalued. See **cheap security**.

sector implied volatility. The volatility implied by prices of nonbullet bonds in a given sector. See **volatility**.

sector yield curve. A yield curve composed of bonds sharing closely similar credit ratings and issuer types.

short an option. Write or sell an option giving the buyer the right to exercise a transaction at a predetermined price range in exchange for paying a premium.

short rate. In the lognormal interest-rate model, the term used to describe any of the individual short-term interest rates composing a given period's interest-rate distribution.

sinking-fund bond. A bond containing a provision allowing the issuer to sink, or pay back to bondholders, portions of the bond's principal periodically before maturity. Sinks may be mandatory, in which case the issuer *must* sink the specified amounts on specified dates, or voluntary, in which the issuer has discretion as to whether a sink will take place.

stochastic. Possessing a random or chaotic characteristic, like the real world. Risk managers tend to prefer such models, but the computational requirements are significantly higher.

strike price. See **exercise price**.

swaptions. Options on forward-starting interest-rate swaps.

term structure of interest rates. The relationship between interest rates and time to maturity, as exhibited by closely similar bonds, such as risk-free Treasury issues.

term structure of volatility (TSOV). The relationship between interest-rate volatility and time to maturity, as exhibited by a particular market sector. Fixed-income option models that require the specification of a term structure of volatility as an input are called TSOV models.

theoretical fair-value analysis. A method of financial analysis that estimates the theoretical value of a particular bond based on the values of closely similar issues.

theoretical zero-coupon rates. See **implied benchmark spot rate**.

time value. The difference between an option's total value (option value) and its intrinsic value. See **intrinsic value**.

underhedged. A condition in which the risk exposure of a hedge position is less than that of the primary position being hedged.

volatility (assumed). The volatility specified as the uncertainty assumption in an option-evaluation model. Most practitioners favor using implied volatilities derived from observed prices of relevant options as the basis for a volatility assumption. Historical volatilities are used when implied values are unavailable or unknown.

volatility curve. See **term structure of volatility**.

volatility (historical). A statistical measure of the variability or uncertainty of a security's value, return, or other performance attribute over a specified historical period. This volatility measure may be computed for any security for which sufficient historical performance data exist and is a measure of past behavior.

volatility (implied). The volatility of an underlying security's performance that is implied by the price and exercise attributes of an option on that security. This volatility measure may be computed only from an option's price and is an indication of the market's expectation about future behavior.

yield. The single interest rate that present-values a designated series of future payments to a given present value. For bonds, the yield is calculated to a designated redemption date, such as maturity or worst call. Also known as "internal rate of return." See **EQUATION 1.1** on page 9.

yield curve. A curve generated by plotting bond yields versus their maturities.

yield spread. The difference between the yields of two bonds.

yields-to-call analysis. An analysis that calculates, for a given price, the yield to each possible future redemption date of a bond.

yield to workout. The yield of a bond to a specified assumed redemption (workout) date.

yield-to-worst analysis. An analysis that calculates, for a given price, the yield to each possible future redemption date of a bond, with the goal of identifying the redemption date with the lowest yield. This is the worst-case yield from an investor's standpoint.

REFERENCES
& ADDITIONAL READING

Berger, Eric, PhD. "Understanding Option-Adjusted Spread Duration." *Bloomberg Magazine,* October 1992. A closer look at risk measures in general and OAS duration in particular.

———, and William Gartland, CFA. "The Bloomberg Corporate Bond OAS Model." Unpublished paper. An in-depth mathematical description of the Bloomberg lognormal model.

Black, Fischer, Emmanuel Dermam, and William Toy. "A One-Factor Model of Interest Rates and Its Application to Treasury Bond Options." *Financial Analysts Journal,* January–February 1990. A straightforward description of a one-factor interest-rate model.

Black, Fischer, and Piotr Karasinski. "Bond and Option Pricing When Short Rates Are Lognormal." *Financial Analysts Journal,* July–August 1991. A description of a one-factor model of bond prices, yields, and options.

Fabozzi, Frank J., and Steven V. Mann. *Floating-Rate Securities.* New York: John Wiley & Sons, Inc., 2000.

Gartland, William, CFA. "Calculating Implied Spot Rates from Benchmark Yields." *Bloomberg Magazine,* November 1992. A description of the various methodologies employed to derive implied spot rates from benchmark yields.

Ho, Thomas S. Y. "Evolution of Interest Rate Models: A Comparison." *The Journal of Derivatives,* Summer 1995. A review of the evolution of interest-rate models.

Hull, John, and Alan White. "New Ways with the Yield Curve." *Risk,* October 1990. A comparison of three interest-rate models.

Koenigsberg, Mark, Janet Showers, and James Streit. "The Term Structure of Volatility and Bond Option Valuation." *The Journal of Fixed Income,* September 1991. An illuminating discussion of bond-option models, with particular attention paid to the use of a time-dependent volatility parameter.

Kopprasch, Robert W. "Option-Adjusted Spread Analysis: Going Down the Wrong Path." *Financial Analysts Journal,* May–June 1994. A discussion of the pitfalls of OAS analysis.

Longstaff, Francis A., and Eduardo S. Schwartz. "Interest Rate Volatility and Bond Prices." *Financial Analysts Journal,* July–August 1993. The effect of changes in bond-market volatility on default-free bonds.

Stigum, Marcia. *Money Market Calculations: Yields, Break-Evens, and Arbitrage.* Homewood, IL: Dow Jones–Irwin, 1981. A detailed, comprehensive treatment of short-term price–interest-rate calculations.

INDEX

About Bloomberg

Bloomberg L.P., founded in 1981, is a global information services, news, and media company. Headquartered in New York, the company has sales and news operations worldwide.

Bloomberg, serving customers on six continents, holds a unique position within the financial services industry by providing an unparalleled range of features in a single package known as the BLOOMBERG PROFESSIONAL® service. By addressing the demand for investment performance and efficiency through an exceptional combination of information, analytic, electronic trading, and Straight Through Processing tools, Bloomberg has built a worldwide customer base of corporations, issuers, financial intermediaries, and institutional investors.

BLOOMBERG NEWS®, founded in 1990, provides stories and columns on business, general news, politics, and sports to leading newspapers and magazines throughout the world. BLOOMBERG TELEVISION®, a 24-hour business and financial news network, is produced and distributed globally in seven languages. BLOOMBERG RADIO℠ is an international radio network anchored by flagship station BLOOMBERG® 1130 (WBBR-AM) in New York.

In addition to the BLOOMBERG PRESS® line of books, Bloomberg publishes *BLOOMBERG MARKETS®* magazine. To learn more about Bloomberg, call a sales representative at:

London:	+44-20-7330-7500
New York:	+1-212-318-2000
Tokyo:	+81-3-3201-8900

FOR IN-DEPTH MARKET INFORMATION and news, visit the Bloomberg Web site at **www.bloomberg.com**, which draws from the news and power of the BLOOMBERG PROFESSIONAL® service and Bloomberg's host of media products to provide high-quality news and information in multiple languages on stocks, bonds, currencies, and commodities.

About the Reviser

Tom Miller, in his role as head of the fixed income and derivatives sales team at Bloomberg L.P. in New York, works every day with some of the world's best bond traders. Additionally, he teaches at the New York University School of Continuing and Professional Studies. Prior to joining Bloomberg, he traded in the money markets for eleven years.